You Can't Teach Leadership, but It Can Be Learned

You Can't Teach LEADERSHIP, but It Can Be LEARNED

An Exploration of the Values of Leaders

Lloyd J. Edwards Jr.

OPEN BOOK
EDITIONS
A Berrett–Koehler Partner

You Can't Teach Leadership, but It Can Be Learned
An Exploration of the Values of Leaders

iUniverse books may be ordered through booksellers or by contacting:

iUniverse
1663 Liberty Drive
Bloomington, IN 47403
www.iuniverse.com
1-800-Authors (1-800-288-4677)

ISBN: 978-1-4759-4942-1 (sc)
ISBN: 978-1-4759-4941-4 (hc)
ISBN: 978-1-4759-4943-8 (e)

Library of Congress Control Number: 2012916492

Printed in the United States of America

iUniverse rev. date: 09/17/2012

Dedication

Many people had a dramatic effect on my life in the twenty years that I was involved with the Supervisory Leadership Program. I will always be grateful to Lieutenant Terry Cunningham, the brains behind the program, for his wisdom, patience, and sharing.

Another great influence on me was Sergeant Gilbert Aguilar of the Los Angeles County Sheriff's Department, who joined our staff as an instructor in 1999. Gil was an excellent addition to our team; however in 2005, Gil was diagnosed with a form of bladder cancer.

The cancer apparently did not know Gil very well, so it was surprised at the fight Gil delivered. Gil went through surgery and chemotherapy. He was cleared of the cancer and was back to work with us in a year.

In 2008, Gil and I were facilitating a class together in the San Diego area. We had a great group of people that bonded from the start. During the fourth month, Gil pulled me aside for lunch; I could tell he was disturbed by something. He said that the cancer had returned and was showing up in various parts of his body. He would need to start treatment and might miss some upcoming sessions. He did not want this information shared with the class; he wanted to continue as long as he could without distracting the group from its mission.

Gil could not make it to the sixth month. He told me he was really taking a beating with the chemotherapy and the outlook was not good. He wanted to spend time with his family and recover. I was forced to break the news to the class on the first morning of that month, and it did not go over well. The group was upset by the news, and many tears were shed before we could get to work; but they did go to work because they did not want to disappoint Gil.

Gil started doing better and returned to finish the class in the seventh and eighth months. At graduation, Gil got up to speak. He thanked me for being his partner and his mentor. He presented me with a fountain pen and told me I had to write a book on leadership. I promised him and the class that I would complete that someday.

Gil called me from his hospital bed on August 23, 2010. He told me he was sorry he had not returned calls or gotten together with me in a while. He said he was really engaged in the fight of his life with his cancer and was going to undergo a new process in a last-ditch effort to control it. On August 27, Gil finally lost his battle with the disease and passed away.

At the funeral, his wonderful wife, Lidia, described Gil as her "missing puzzle piece." Los Angeles County Sheriff Lee Baca spoke about what a giving person Gil was and explained that he had taught an inmate leadership program at the jail, which was designed to help develop good values and ethical behavior among the inmates. He had also been involved in the Deputy Leadership Program to help young officers in the Sheriff's Department. Gil was a strong man, jam-packed full of all the leadership qualities discussed in this book. Heaven is a better place with the addition of Gil Aguilar.

This effort is dedicated to honor Gilbert Aguilar (January 3, 1952–August 27, 2010), a leader, a hero, and my friend. A Titus man to the end: "Likewise, exhort the young men to be sober minded in all things showing yourself to be a pattern of good works; in doctrine showing integrity, reverence, incorruptibility, sound speech that cannot be condemned" (Titus 2:6–8).

Lloyd Edwards
Huntington Beach, California
2012

Contents

Introduction

You Can't Teach Leadership, but It Can Be Learned rests on the premise that leadership is a value-based trait. The best leaders have values such as compassion, honesty, forgiveness, kindness, flexibility, and tenacity. These are values that you cannot teach, but that people learn through life experiences. Leaders combine values with skills such as the ability to delegate, teach, inspire, manage time, and communicate vision. It is this combination of the art of leadership and the science of management that produces the quality leader who is capable of inspiring followers.

This book is an exploration of leadership values in combination with management skills that have never been presented in such an understandable format. It is written to help leaders at all levels: from the CEO down to section leaders, and from PTA presidents to parents. I believe it will have an impact on the life of the reader both personally and professionally.

The book is a personal journey through the values of a leader and how they apply to you. The design of the book comes from a program I was involved in for nearly twenty years. This program began in about 1986 when a lieutenant from the Los Angeles Police Department, Terry Cunningham, designed a course for California's Commission on Peace Officer Standards and Training (POST) to improve leadership. The program was called the Supervisory Leadership Institute (SLI). In 1996, Lieutenant Cunningham was presented with the POST Award for Excellence in Training for this program.

The SLI program was a very intense course of study. It was a new way of teaching through facilitation and learning that is reflected in this book. The course consisted of three-day workshops each month, spread out over eight months with participants reading a minimum of fourteen books. The design was an experiential learning event where the students were active learning partners in the process. Learning goals were covered in a flexible order, visited and revisited in different formats as we moved through the concepts of leadership in a dynamic and fluid manner.

I was one of the initial instructors in the program. I also spent thirty years leading and managing in law enforcement, including working as the operations manager for an FAA repair and hangar facility for the police department, where I managed flight operations, pilots, aircraft, leases, purchases, and maintenance.

It took me years to really understand the way these concepts of leadership are woven together and the value of presenting them in this manner. I want you to explore your opinions and perspectives, and challenge the concepts as they are presented. The key to learning is dialogue—not discussion. In discussion, we attempt to change a point of view to match ours. In dialogue we collectively attempt to find the truth, despite our perspectives. In order to participate in learning, we must suspend our assumptions or paradigms, which tell us we are correct in our current thinking.

I ask that we respect each other as colleagues and be open to other perspectives as this progresses. There will be times when you wonder where this is going, but be patient and trust that it will come together. We will discuss a concept and move on to another without closure. This is a method designed to create a deeper understanding of the concepts as we discover how they apply to our own paradigms and fit into a larger perspective. Leaving discussions open will show how concepts are interconnected to each other.

Picture something similar to a spiderweb to illustrate how interconnected the matrix of leadership is. Each concept is covered and tied to another until the matrix is so interwoven that you cannot look at one section without thinking of how it is connected to all the others. Lieutenant Cunningham described it as Eastern versus Western thinking: a view of the whole versus a view of each individual part.

There is nothing new about leadership. These are timeless principles that have been around for thousands of years. In writing this book, I am trying to capture the essence of leadership—or maybe the science of it—while also attempting to show the art. It is really challenging to learn leadership from a book alone. I do believe this book will be a rewarding experience that will help you to grasp the concepts of leadership while opening the door to learn. I believe this subject requires experiential learning, as in a completely involved personal experience where you can be challenged openly and inwardly about your thoughts and actions. You may accomplish this if you use this book to its full potential.

Together we carefully progress through stages that will encourage you to take a deep internal look at your values to see how they match the values we hold dear to leadership. This self-examination process will help you choose ways you can reprioritize your own value system to understand and learn leadership.

Hopefully, it will create thoughts that cause you to challenge your values, and motivations to help improve your abilities as a leader. It may also reassure you that your values and motivations are good and you are on track as a leader.

Each chapter references two or more books. They are briefly noted in the chapters to help support the concepts. In the course, this reading was required prior to each workshop. Some of the references are well-known works on leadership; the connection of some of the others to leadership and management may surprise you. I believe that reading the referenced books and articles and watching the recommended movies can make this book a more effective tool for learning leadership.

This is not a how-to book. So much varies with circumstances, conditions, and changing environments that the answers could never cover all events or situations. This is not a process by which you will memorize correct answers, if any even exist. This book is designed to lead you to examine your own thought processes and discover the abilities that lie within you to solve problems. My hope is that through the exploration of leadership concepts, values, and traits, you may come to understand what is required for others to consider you one of the best leaders they have ever known. Putting that into practice will be up to you.

On the first day of a class, I always asked participants to tell me what they had heard about the course. I got a lot of responses about it being too hard, very intense, mind opening, repetitive, boring, and challenging; some past participants said that they had received some good tools and so forth. My response was always that if graduates said that they had learned and now knew everything about leadership, they had failed. If they told you that they had learned a lot about themselves and that all knowledge is incomplete, they had been successful.

All experiences in life are what you make of them. Your own desire to learn is all important. This is an exploration of value identification and leadership concepts. I don't claim to be all knowing or have all the answers, but I studied, practiced, and presented the material for many years. I saw successes and failures, both mine and those of others, which caused me to come to the opinion that *you can't teach leadership, but it can be learned*!

Chapter One

Identifying the Barriers for Leaders

While on a plane returning from teaching a session in Sacramento, I noticed the guy next to me was reading *The 7 Habits of Highly Effective People*, by Dr. Stephen R. Covey.[1] Since the book was being used in our leadership program, I asked him if he liked the book. He said yes, and then went on to explain to me that he was a "leadership consultant" who gave one-day seminars on how to be a leader. He thought the book might add some insight to his course. I told him that I was a presenter in a leadership program also and that we used the Covey book in our course. He said he thought that was great. He asked if maybe I could help him understand this thing Covey called a "par-a-dig-um." I explained that the word was pronounced "pair-a-dime" and went on to discuss it with him. What I soon realized was that this guy did not have a good understanding of leadership or what he was teaching. I also realized our program was something very different and really special.

Over the years, I have come across lots of folks teaching leadership. It seems everyone wants to get into the leadership teaching game. There are a lot of perspectives and a lot of quick fixes that promise to teach you the skills required to be a good leader. If these promises are true, and if leadership is so teachable, then it should follow that all the people who have been to leadership training are great leaders. But we all know people

---

[1] Covey, Stephen R., *The 7 Habits of Highly Effective People* (New York: Simon and Shuster, 1989).

who have been to training and returned worse than they were before they went. We continue to witness incident after incident of failed leadership with examples that include Enron, Countrywide, Lehman Brothers, law enforcement, state and federal governments, and so on. It seems that everyone is still starving and searching for good leadership.

I have been involved with leadership training for over twenty years. I have presented many classes, and have researched and practiced the art of leadership in a number of situations. After all of the time I have put into learning and training in leadership, I am doubtful that it is being taught with any reasonable success. That is because I believe leadership is a value-based trait, and unless someone is willing to challenge their values, they cannot learn good leadership. Leadership is a complex combination of particular character traits, skills, and basic values that tend to make successful leaders.

It is obvious that people learn certain values, qualities, and skills as they grow. Individuals, such as parents and friends, as well as institutions, like churches and schools, all try to teach values and influence us. This works for some, making them the special types of people who are capable of leading. For others this doesn't work so well, and they learn values, traits, and skills that will insure they will not be good leaders. We all learn values, and we all have our own perspectives regarding their importance. This is what leadership training should be designed to do: identify and challenge values, giving people an opportunity to learn what is required to lead.

A leader has a moral sense of values, always strives to do the right thing, and does not compromise for selfish reasons. A leader keeps an eye on the vision/mission but never loses sight of the coworkers that he or she cares for. A leader shows confidence that together we can prevail. A leader always has the courage to do what is necessary for the good of all, without casting aside the value of the one. A leader is not boastful or arrogant, but kind, compassionate, and inspiring. A leader is not afraid to ask forgiveness. Leaders do not act out of emotion, but create it. Leaders always listen more than they talk.

I believe that much of the current leadership training is like the movie *Tin Men*.[2] *Tin Men* was a comedy about aluminum roofing salesmen who pushed a product they knew little about and used any method they could to sell it. Sadly, leadership training today sometimes resembles the aluminum roofing market depicted in the film; it may be the "Tin Roof" market of this time.

I have met with many folks involved in leadership training. One person has written several books and teaches one- and two-day seminars. On one occasion, he met with our program instructors. He admitted that there is nothing really new in leadership and that a one- or two-day program is completely ineffective. He said it was just what everyone was doing, and he was making really good money at it. He also said that organizations are just not willing to take the time and make the necessary commitments to really help people learn leadership. I was excited about his honesty, but he is still out there doing the same thing.

Some would say that leadership is nothing more than a set of skills that can be easily taught. James Kouzes and Barry Posner are renowned authors in the field and said this about leadership: "The truth is that leadership is an observable set of skills and abilities that are useful whether one is in the executive suite or on the front line, on Wall Street or on Main Street." [3]

They go on to talk about strengthening these skills and suggest that leadership is not the property of a select few who can understand the mystery. But maybe what they are talking about is really management skills, not leadership.

Is leadership a skill or an art? Would you say leadership is extrinsic or intrinsic? Can you teach intrinsic values? There are some mystical ingredients we find in good leaders, and this is what we are seeking to explore. I believe they are identifiable and learnable, just not teachable in the traditional sense.

---

[2] *Tin Men*, Touchstone Pictures, 1987.
[3] Kouzes, James M. and Posner, Barry Z., *A Leader's Legacy* (San Francisco: Jossey-Bass A. Wiley, 2006), 118.

Most people would look at leadership as an art form because it is so difficult to place into a scientific box. How exactly do you measure leadership in any organization? If it were just a set of skills, then we could send out a manual, and all you would have to do to learn how to lead would be read the manual. Reading a lot of golf books does not make one a good golfer. This does not mean that a person is not capable of becoming a good golfer or that the books will not help.

If you attend a seminar in which someone starts telling you they are some great leadership guru who can teach you all there is to know about leadership, you may want to be very cautious. I would just ask for a refund and leave because that ability—to teach leadership in that way—does not exist.

It would be completely arrogant for me to say that I can teach leadership. It is arrogant to think you can teach anyone anything that they are not willing to learn. In the end it is always your choice to learn or not. By facilitating and exploring leadership principles, I have seen people learn leadership. It was not me that taught them; they learned by self-induced, experiential learning that came through examining their own lives, values, and paradigms.

Most of us think we pretty much know the way things operate. We are set in our views of how the world operates and resent anyone telling us we are wrong. I am always amazed when I try to explain something to my kids and they tell me "I know!" I get frustrated and ask, "How could you know? You have never seen that before!"

It is not possible to teach something to someone if they think they already know it. I dealt with many officers in the police department who thought that after three years, they had seen everything (I was one of them at one time). Then, something happens, and you discover how wrong you were. You suddenly realize you don't know it all. You chalk that one up to experience and assume that surely you will have seen everything or know everything in five, ten, twenty, or thirty years—only to discover that all knowledge is incomplete and you will never really know much for sure.

Many times along the way, older, more experienced officers would try to tell us things, but we ignored them, because we thought we already knew how it was. Maybe that is why our kids are frustrating; we want to save them the pain we went through, but they refuse to listen. Robert Pirsig tells us, "The truth stands at the door and knocks, but we say go away, I'm searching for the truth."[4] While I will tell you I cannot teach you leadership, I do believe that leadership can be learned, and I think I can help.

There is clearly a difference between leadership and management that we will need to explore. We also need to explore how we look at leadership and what it means to different people with different perspectives. Are leaders courageous or cowardly? What is honor, and do leaders have it? Do organizations need it? Must leaders live moral lives? Are leaders sensitive to the feelings of others, or is that a weak trait? Do employees love, fear, or respect their leaders? Do leaders care what happens to the folks they work with? Do leaders have "grandeur and nobility of spirit?"[5] Are these things teachable or learnable? Are these traits that you possess?

How Do You See It?

So let's start exploring with our first look into paradigms. A paradigm is a compilation of one's values, experiences, education, prejudices, biases, fears, imaginations, and desires. It makes up our expectations of how we think things should operate. In short, it is our view of the world as we think it is.

Paradigms are like opinions; basically, everybody has them. Our paradigms may not be correct by some standards; but they are certainly ours, and we definitely own them. Try to challenge someone's paradigm, and you may be in for a fight! When it comes down to the way we think things are, we are pretty resistant to anyone trying to change us. We can go to great lengths to justify, rationalize, and even fantasize to maintain our paradigms.

---

[4] Pirsig, Robert M., *Zen and the Art of Motorcycle Maintenance* (New York: Bantam Books, William Morrow and Company, 1975), 5.

[5] Machiavelli, Niccolo, *The Prince*, 1532, translation by Luigi Ricci, 1903, (New York: Oxford University Press, 1921).

Blink by Malcolm Gladwell[6] does a good job of exploring paradigms, how they are formed, and what results from them. Some of the results are good and some are not so good. We get ideas fixed in our heads about how things should be, how things will happen, what is the right way or wrong way, what is normal and abnormal, the proper sequence of events, and so on. Gladwell uses an example of a museum curator who views a piece and just has an inner feeling it is not correct, even though the documentation shows it to be proper. In another example, a police officer views a series of events and takes action based on his inner feelings that an immediate danger exists. The curator's feelings turn out to be correct, but the officer's result in a catastrophic outcome. Both are good examples of the way values and experiences play into our view of the world and contribute to our responses.

Paradigms can change, so let's look at a couple of stories that demonstrate the effects and the process. First, imagine that you are at work and you see an employee being rude to a client. The employee's manager immediately calls him into her office to ask why he was so rude to one of your best customers. The employee is nonresponsive, appears dazed by the inquiry, and just sits with his head down. His manager demands an answer as the employee looks up with tears in his eyes. He tells the manager that his wife died suddenly of a heart attack the previous night. He says that he has been up all night making arrangements but did not know what to do with himself this morning, so he just came to work.

This extra bit of information does not fit anyone's expectations of the situation and paradigm of the event. Suddenly, a severe change results, and everyone becomes embarrassed and sympathetic to this employee. The situation is no longer upsetting, but instead becomes extremely sad and understandable. Everything else would now be placed on hold to help him deal with this tragedy. This tale might be similar to any number of events in which you or I have made a comment only to end up with our foot in our mouths.

Chief Petty Officer Frank Koch Jr. related a paradigm-shifting story about a battleship, a captain, and a seaman in the US Navy's magazine *Proceedings*

---

6 Gladwell, Malcolm, *Blink, The Power of Thinking Without Thinking* (New York: Little, Brown and Co, 2005).

(Dr. Covey shares this story also in *7 Habits...*). In this story a lookout on a battleship spots a light off the bow during low visibility. He notifies the captain that the ship is on a possible collision course with another vessel. The captain tells a signalman to signal the other vessel and have it alter its course. The signalman does this but gets a quick reply from the source of the light that he should immediately alter his course. The captain is annoyed and tells the signalman to tell the other vessel to alter its course— he is a captain! The person responding indicates that he is a seaman, and he recommends the captain immediately alter his course. The captain becomes very upset and identifies himself as the captain of a battleship and tells the seaman to change his course, demanding the seaman identify his vessel. The seaman replies that he is a seaman in a lighthouse.

You would think any captain would see the error of his ways and alter course, but there is a problem associated with paradigms and people— ego and arrogance. Information like what the captain received should be sufficient to create a paradigm change in every case, but in 1985 the aircraft carrier USS *Enterprise* ran aground after the executive officer and crew tried repeatedly to warn the captain of the impending danger.

This is a small introduction to paradigms. They can be called different things in different materials (patterns, models, philosophical-theoretical frameworks, discipline, and so on), but the descriptions are similar. We seem to be locked into our paradigms, and we resist change. I believe that is because our paradigms go to our basic values, our most deeply held beliefs. In order to learn, we need to understand them, be able to suspend them, and allow in other thoughts, perspectives, and ideas.

The Sundance Kid

The movie *Butch Cassidy and the Sundance Kid*[7] includes a scene in which Sundance is at a table in a saloon, playing poker with several cowboys, including one fella who really thinks he is a tough guy. Sundance wins several hands, and the tough guy accuses him of being a cheat. He tells Sundance that he can leave, but "the money stays." Sundance takes

---

[7] *Butch Cassidy and the Sundance Kid*, Twentieth Century Fox, 1969.

exception to being called a cheat, as Butch comes in to get him to leave. Butch tries unsuccessfully to smooth over the situation, suggesting the other player ask the two of them to stay, but he gets pushed aside by the tough guy. Butch then says, "I can't help you, Sundance." As Sundance clears his coat from his sidearm, the tough guy suddenly realizes *he has just accused the Sundance Kid of cheating.*

Well, right about now the tough guy is experiencing a paradigm change as he says, "I didn't know you were the Sundance Kid when I said you were cheating. If I draw on you, you'll kill me." Sundance responds, "There is that possibility." Butch quickly jumps in, warning, "No, you'd be killing yourself." Butch continues with, "So why don't you just ask us to stay?" After some coaxing, the tough guy asks them to stay, dropping any suggestion of cheating, and Butch and Sundance begin to leave. The tough guy still doesn't quite get it, though. He asks, "Just how good are you, Kid?" Butch dives for cover as Sundance turns, draws and fires, shooting the gun out of the tough guy's holster, and then continues firing at the pistol, knocking it across the room.

So what happened here? A tiny bit of new information was introduced that changed the way the tough guy viewed the world. We need to explore this a bit to understand what is at work. If paradigms are values, experiences, prejudices, and fears, did any of that change with the introduction of the Sundance Kid in the scenario?

My point here is not to tell you the answer (if there is a correct answer to this question), but this is where you start to become involved in this book as a learning partner. We need to explore and think about how these things occur to be able to understand how we think and define our paradigm or view of the world. As I said in the beginning, I do not believe we can teach leadership, but I do believe we can learn leadership. We can choose to enhance or implement changes in our paradigms that will allow us to become more effective leaders.

What does the poker player value? How would you prioritize his values of money, wealth, pride, courage, life, respect, kindness, and compassion before the disclosure that he was facing the Sundance Kid? How about after? Did his view of the value of life (that is, his own life) change—maybe get shuffled up to the top of the list? Where was pride in that list before? After? Was he courageous when he thought he was the faster gun, and a coward when his understanding of things changed?

Did his values change, or did he go through a major reorganization/ reprioritization of his paradigm? This appears to have been a learning experience that came with some humility and discomfort and that might affect all his future encounters—or at least those that involve playing poker with strangers!

How can we change or examine our paradigms without getting shot by the Sundance Kid or someone else? Can we avoid an embarrassing moment at work that gets everyone talking about the stupid stunt we tried to pull, or even worse, a law enforcement agent taking us out the door in handcuffs? Is it as simple as saying, "Maybe I don't know everything" and listening intently to those older voices that are trying to save us some pain in learning?

In every class I have facilitated, participants have come in expressing their expectations that they will listen to new ideas and concepts, and learn by accepting other perspectives. However, by 2:00 p.m. on the first day, after a few exercises, all of that is shot to heck. They revert back and try to impose their own paradigms on others, since of course, they know just how it all should be.

By 4:00 p.m. participants were usually arguing with the facilitators, refusing to accept any other thoughts and ideas—until they were slapped in the face with the expectations they had written down in the early morning. Suddenly they realized (the aha moment) that they had become everything they had come to the class to argue against. This epiphany, paradigm change, or aha moment—call it what you will—is that embarrassing moment when you realize you are the problem. This is where learning occurs. You realize the necessity to do something good leaders always do, constantly challenge and re-evaluate their paradigm.

Is There a Difference between Leaders and Managers?

Simply put, *yes, there is a difference between leaders and managers.* Many look on the good leader as the person who picks up the flag and rallies the troops to take the hill in the face of grave danger, never fearing for himself as he charges on. That may be one limited example of leadership, but leaders lead every day and in much broader circumstances. In the television miniseries *Band of Brothers,*[8] Sergeant (later Major) Winters led during battle but also led every day through his examples of courage, honor, and compassion. Steve Jobs led at Apple. He was so recognized as the company's leader that the stock dropped dramatically on rumors of his poor health.

Peter Drucker is largely considered to be the father of modern management theory. His 1954 book *The Practice of Management* was the first one we used in background study for the leadership course. Even though it was written in 1954 and some of the stories are now outdated, it contains the basic designs of management we are still using and talking about today. Many of Drucker's thoughts have been modified and redesigned by nearly everyone who has written about management. In this book, Drucker says, "Leaders are born[9]." He goes on to describe certain leadership traits and how important leadership is to an organization, but he bounces back and forth between describing traits of a leader and describing a good manager.

To start looking into the differences between leaders and managers, describe the best leader you ever worked for. Start listing things such as truthfulness, caring, strong principles, honesty, trustworthiness, good communication skills, vision, intellect, humor, thoughtfulness, compassion, competence, consistency, fairness, and unselfishness. Now describe the worst leader you ever worked for. How about such qualities as selfishness, untrustworthiness, incompetence, micromanagement,

---

[8] *Band of Brothers*, a ten-part miniseries based on the book by Stephen E. Ambrose, was produced by Steven Spielberg, Tom Hanks, Preston Smith, Erik Jendresen, and Stephen E. Ambrose for HBO.

[9] Drucker, Peter, *The Practice of Management* (New York: Harper and Row Publishing, 1954).

rudeness, cronyism, abruptness, anger, meanness, inflexibility, lack of caring, stubbornness, wishy-washiness, and unpredictability?

Let us look at the traits of a manager. Have you heard the acronym POSDCORB?[10] It refers to the responsibilities of a manager and stands for planning, organizing, staffing, directing, co-ordinating, reporting, and budgeting. You can probably think of many more management skills, so add them to your list.

Do you see a difference in the descriptions of leaders and managers? The management skills are teachable skills for the most part. The leadership traits are all value based. They are things that make up your personality. How do we teach someone to care about others, to be truthful, trustworthy, honest, compassionate, and unselfish?

A first statement about leadership: *Leadership is value based and unselfish.* It is not about creating a legacy or getting people to like you by being nice to them. It is about your values being observed and interpreted by others who choose to follow.

You can be a good manager and a poor leader or a good leader and a poor manager. A good leader might lead the team to the top of a hill or the end of a project, but forget to plan for enough food, water, ammunition, long-term support, and contracts to hold the position. Or a good manager might get the team everything they need but be unable to motivate them to get up the hill because they don't want to follow.

In order to be a "great leader" you are going to need many skills, traits, and values that are recognizable to everyone. In class, we break up into groups to separate these out. For our purposes here, I want to use a couple of examples. You can expand this and make your own list.

---

[10] Gulick, Luther, "Notes on the Theory of Organization," New York: Institute of Public Administration in papers on the Science of Administration, ed. Luther Gulick and L. Urwick, 1937 p. 13.

Skills	**Traits**	**Values**
Organization	Compassionate	Honesty
Scheduling	Supportive	Courage
Delegation	Focused	Humility
Planning	Flexible	Integrity
Technical ability	Understanding	Respectfulness
Training	Communicative	Empathy
Financial	Sense of humor	Reliability
Tactical ability	Assertive	Developer of others

These are *all necessary* skills, traits, and values of a good leader. Some traits and values on this list may be interchangeable or overlap with each other, but they are all things that a good leader needs to be effective. Take something out, such as honesty or compassion, and you begin to lose the others.

Some of these can be categorized as extrinsic skills, things that can be taught and learned, practiced and improved upon. These can be compared to the science portion of management or leadership. The other parts are intrinsic in nature. These things may not be teachable, but we sure know if someone has them or not. These may be what make up the art of leadership.

As we progress, you will see how these are all interconnected in a good leader and impossible to teach by traditional methods. We can teach what is involved in honesty and compassion, but we cannot teach someone to *be* honest or compassionate. Can someone learn honesty or compassion? I think they can, but it requires going back to the paradigms we were discussing. It requires a paradigm change, or something usually associated with a meaningful, life-changing event.

To experience that change, something must occur. Morris Massey did some exploration in value programming and refers to a SEE (significant emotional event) as something that can cause a paradigm change. In the example I gave from *Butch Cassidy and the Sundance Kid*, the SEE was the tough guy's realization that he was dealing with the Sundance Kid, he had made a major mistake, and he was about to die. SEEs tend to be very painful lessons. Not necessarily physically painful or fatal, but emotionally painful or career-killing events.

Sociologist Morris Massey is a unique character. He produced a series of presentations, starting with *What You Are Is Where You Were When.*[11] The purpose was to show that we learn values from periods of time through which we developed. Massey claims we learn these values in our younger years, and they are pretty much set by age fourteen.

He discusses how values are programmed by certain time periods in history. He notes that folks who grew up in the 1930s and suffered through the Depression are savers who require security. In the 1940s, people began to experience mobility and a world war. The 1950s marked a change to the beginning of prosperity, overindulged kids, television, and rock and roll, on through the sixties, seventies, eighties, and so on.

Massey talks a mile a minute. He is exhausting to follow but fun to watch. He makes very excellent points in his presentation, and I recommend watching his video as part of a study in leadership. It can help you understand yourself and begin to identify and change things you don't care for.

During the leadership program, we tried to use exercises to create SEEs for the students but without the experiences becoming things that would hang a permanent jacket on them in the workplace or in their personal lives.

To avoid a painful SEE, we need to focus on the examination of our values and perspectives. To make those paradigm shifts, we have to be totally honest with ourselves first and admit that we have shortcomings and prejudices and that there are things we don't know. If we can admit we don't have a good view of a situation, we might be able to reprioritize our values without facing down the Sundance Kid in a life-or-death drama!

The Massey studies are a tool to learn about ourselves. If we are open to watching, listening, and evaluating ourselves as Massey explains his

---

[11] Massey, Morris, *What You Are Is Where You Were When*, 1976.

perspective on values, we can certainly learn. If you are unwilling to examine your own paradigm, you may be unwilling and unable to learn.

In one of my classes, I had a student who was pretty difficult. After viewing the Massey presentation, he said he was angry. He felt Massey had not included him and his generation in the timeline. The entire class was bewildered by his statements. They felt he was being defensive and refusing to acknowledge that he, not the presentation, might be the problem. The discussion degenerated quickly; several folks in the class became fed up and were pretty blunt with this individual. He eventually left his seat and sat on the floor in the corner of the room facing the wall. It was just incredible; he put himself in time-out rather than face other perspectives! You cannot teach people who refuse to be open to learning, as this person was, but the episode was an enormously impactful learning experience for the rest of the class.

Management and Values

You may have been exposed to tests to determine your management style, for example Smalley and Trent's animal model (are you an Otter or a Lion?), Binder's driver/expressive model, the DiSC profiles, or Keirsey's temperament sorter. All attempt to identify values and determine what management or leadership style you may prefer.

I like the Managerial Values Profile tool by Dr. Marshall Sashkin.[12] This tool gives you some idea of what values are in play as you make decisions in your management style. Dr. Sashkin uses three categories: utilitarian, moral rights, and justice.

Do you make your decisions based on the overall good of the many, as opposed to the one (utilitarian); the individual's personal rights (moral rights); or the belief that all things should be distributed "fairly" over the group (justice)? Like all the tools and theories we see, we look at this as something that can help us understand ourselves and our motivations for making the decisions that we make. Most of these are available to examine online.

---

[12] Sashkin, Marshall, PhD, MVP (Organization Design and Development Inc, 1986).

In the course, we asked students to review a selection process for an assignment. The three choices were worded so as to invoke the differences in utilitarian, moral rights, and justice values. Despite their claims to be open to other perspectives, we saw everyone revert back to the paradigm he or she came with. Some folks, in their explanations of how they made their choices, actually inserted words and phrases into the document that were not there. They did this to support their perspectives and reasoning. It is amazing how the filters in our minds work, causing us to see things that are not there and completely block out things that are. (You can review a sample selection process for yourself at the end of this chapter; make a choice and play along.)

The exercise generally turned into a big argument, with some yelling and very strong positions, until the facilitator stepped in to ask why everyone had become so upset over a make-believe exercise. At that point I redirected the exercise so it became a self-evaluation tool. We began to examine the values that were involved in the selection, and how we (and others) make choices based on similar values and our perceptions of fairness. This allowed us to explore how we make choices and prefer to pick people that share our values, even at the expense of others who may be more deserving.

If we want to say that a good leader is fair and understanding, takes others' feelings into account, can see all sides of the issue, is compassionate, and so on, then all of the values we personally take into account when making decisions need to be reviewed and understood. *Fair* is a term that will be different to everyone, depending on their values and priorities.

We can't be afraid to admit that we have a prejudice or value issue in some area, whether our issues are people of other races or ethnicities, different styles of dress, sexual orientations, or religion, and so on. All of these values are ours to understand and deal with. Once we can face them, admit them, and acknowledge them, we can put them aside and control them. This helps us to suspend our paradigms and be more open to learning other perspectives. Understanding ourselves is key to making us better leaders.

Can You Choose to Change Your Values?

Stimulus versus response is a widely accepted theory in psychology. It basically refers to the carrot-and-stick mentality studied by Pavlov. It is the idea that people respond like animals. If you offer the dog a treat, he will salivate and learn to roll over. You offer a person some reward, and they will react for you. If a certain stimulus is introduced, a person will react in a way that can be predictable, based on his or her experience or on past events. This idea relieves people of responsibility, saying that we basically have no choice in the matter and we are preprogrammed to act a certain way.

The philosophical theory of determinism says that you don't have a choice in your response to a stimulus. Determinism is divided into three categories:

- **Psychic:** My Grandparents did this to me by heritage. So, for example, if you have an Italian background, then you must be "hot blooded" and have an uncontrollable temper.
- **Behavioral**: My parents did it to me. If you were abused by your parents, then you will be an abusive parent. If your father beat your mother, then you will beat your wife or accept that as normal behavior from your husband.
- **Environmental:** My surroundings, my job, my wife, or what have you did it to me. If you had a bad day at work, then you must come home in a bad mood. If the dishwasher breaks, you must get mad and kick the dog, slap your child, get drunk, or the like.

The difference between humans and animals is really more than height, weight, and fur. We have the ability to reason and make choices based on a variety of information. If we take a polar bear from the arctic and place it in the desert, it will probably die. If we take a human and place him or her in the arctic, the person will die—if they don't start thinking and adapt as the Eskimos did. We have the ability to choose a response to any given situation. While Massey says, some preprogramming is in all of us, we still can choose our response.

Viktor E. Frankl's book, *Man's Search for Meaning*,[13] is about having choices in life. Frankl's book was the second book we used in session one of the leadership course as background study. He relates some very unique stories of his time in the concentration camps in Germany during WWII and of a different philosophy called logotherapy that correlates to some values and traits necessary for leadership.

Frankl describes the Jewish prisoners' responses to the guards during WWII and their responses to unavoidable suffering. He tells us we are not helpless and we can choose our response to whatever situation comes before us. He gives great insight as to how he and others were able to cope when they lost everything and the future appeared to be dark. They chose not to allow the Germans to take away hope and the meaning of their lives even though they could take away their lives.

Dave Carey wrote, *The Ways We Choose*,[14] about his experiences as a POW in Vietnam. He wrote about experiences very similar to the ones Frankl did and about how he and the other POWs were able to survive in the face of unavoidable suffering. They did it by choosing to survive. Charlie Plumb wrote about the same thing in his book, *I'm No Hero*[15] (though he clearly is one, as are Dave Carey and everyone else that fought to survive). It is a recurring theme among leaders, survivors, and heroes.

When we are faced with a situation, we can choose our response. I decide what response to give, it is called being responsible, or *response-able*, able to choose my actions and, even more deeply, my values.

In 2011, a story came out of the Atlanta school system (reported by the governor's office), which revealed that 178 named teachers had been caught cheating. They were changing students' grades to make it appear that they had done better on tests than they actually had. The teachers

---

[13] Frankl, Viktor E., *Man's Search for Meaning: An Introduction into Logo Therapy* (New York: Touchstone Edition, 1984).

[14] Carey, Dave, *The Ways We Choose: Lessons from a POW's Experience* (Wilsonville, OR: Book Partners, 2000).

[15] Plumb, Charlie, *I'm No Hero* (Mechanicsburg, PA: Executive Books, 1973).

claimed the reason was that the underperforming school would lose federal funds under the No Child Left Behind Act. Therefore, if the students did not improve, they could lose their jobs. Folks were choosing a response to a stimulus, although it was probably not a good one. They were blaming the legislation, saying that it gave them no choice and had basically forced them to cheat! Did they make a choice based on their values?

Argue for your weaknesses, and they are yours! We must accept that we have the ability to choose and determine our own paths; we have the freedom to choose, and no one can take that away. Helplessness is not a leadership trait. If you say you can't, then you are probably right. If you refuse to accept responsibility for your own acts, how can you hold others accountable for theirs? People do not want to work for a leader who says, "Do as I say, not as I do." These attitudes do not instill confidence or create followers.

As we discussed this in class, we would wander into the application of choice to drug addiction, alcoholism, child abuse, domestic violence, and so on. It is an interesting topic that brings out a variety of opinions. Have these issues been deemed medical issues in order to support a drug industry, a medical industry, and a psychological industry? Is this just a problem of people who do not have the will to accept responsibility for their problems? The classes' explorations often drifted into discussions of whether someone growing up in a gang-infested ghetto knows it is wrong to steal.

In Charles Sykes' book, *A Nation of Victims, the Decay of the American Character*,[16] Sykes goes into detail explaining how he believes that Americans have been convinced that all these disorders are disabling illnesses that require medical and psychological treatment. I cannot provide answers to these questions, but the purpose of the dialogue is to explore the idea that we have control over—and choice in—our responses.

Do you ever talk about the employee you were unable to save? Was it your responsibility to save them? Or was it your responsibility to hold

---

[16] Sykes, Charles J., *A Nation of Victims: The Decay of the American Character* (New York: St. Martin's Press, 1992).

them accountable for their behavior so they could save themselves? We tend to want to help people, and as leaders we should help. But we do not want to steal responsibility away from them; they have their own choices to make.

Our job as leaders is to help them understand that they have choices and there are consequences for those choices. The leader's job is to show them the options and provide care and encouragement. It becomes very frustrating when they fail, but if you have done your job, the failures are theirs. That does not mean we do not forgive when it is a learning event. There are many circumstances that will play into second chances ("It is neither American nor Christian to nag a repentant sinner to his grave," said Admiral James Stockdale, commander of the POWs in Vietnam[17]), but that is a discussion for another chapter.

There are not a lot of things we have control over in this world, but our response to stimulus is one. Dr. Covey talks about our areas of control in his book, *The 7 Habits,* and refers to our circles of influence and our circles of concern.[18] This concept simply means that we each have our areas of influence, which are those things we have control over, and our areas of concern, things we are concerned about but can't control.

If you really think about it, we don't have much control over anything except ourselves. That brings us back to Frankl and all the others who talk about the choice each of us has about how we proactively address stimulus.

We control nothing but our actions. Our actions may involve holding others accountable, setting rules, or enforcing rules, performance measures, and policies. We do not have control over others' responses, but we do have control over the consequences of not meeting our expectations.

---

[17] Manning, Robert, *The World of Epictetus: Reflections on Survival and Leadership* (Boston: Atlantic Monthly Company, 1978), 297.

[18] Covey, Stephen R., *The 7 Habits of Highly Effective People* (New York: Simon and Shuster, 1989), 81–88.

Our areas of concern involve a lot of stuff. I am concerned about the value of the dollar, the colors of paint we use on the police cars, the war abroad, the national debt, the contract we are negotiating, the material presented in school, my future promotions, and a host of other things. Most of that is way out of my control. I can control what I invest in; I can write a memo about the color of the paint; I can write or call my representative in Congress; I can run for the negotiating team or board of directors, study for promotion, and go back to school. There are ways I can expand my influence, but concentrating on things I have no control over will tend to cause me frustration and heartburn.

Instead, I choose to be proactive, operating in my area of influence and hoping that, by doing the best I can, others will begin to take notice. Will I eventually expand that area of influence to include others? Is that how leadership happens? Is that how Gandhi and Mother Teresa became such influential leaders?

The opposite of being proactive is being reactive. We should not let circumstances control our responses. We are not helpless in our responses to whatever situations present themselves. We don't have to wait for things to happen to us; if you can predict it, you can prevent it. I have flown aircraft for many years. I was a pilot and commander of the helicopter unit at the Huntington Beach Police Department for ten years. One thing I learned is that the pilot in command is responsible for everything. If the rotors fall off the aircraft, it is your fault. If you choose to deviate from air traffic control instructions, it is your responsibility, and you will be held accountable. Ultimately, you are the only one in control of your actions and the actions of the aircraft.

In the leadership program, we did case studies by watching movies and discussing how they applied to concepts we were exploring. The first movie I used was *Amazing Grace and Chuck*.[19] It explores choice, the power of one person expanding influence to lead others, paradigms, being proactive rather than reactive, and values.

---

[19] *Amazing Grace and Chuck*, Tri-Star Pictures, 1987.

The movies we watched in class were not used for entertainment; they were used as learning tools. Probably the best thing about *Amazing Grace and Chuck* was that it was a simple movie, almost made for an audience of children. Adults may tend to view the film as a joke, but once we started discussing it in class, the participants quickly found that there was a lot of learning available from this movie. The hidden or ignored learning concepts became "aha" experiences in themselves, which helped to work in all the concepts we discuss in chapter 1.

Amazing Grace and Chuck is a fictional movie about a twelve-year-old boy named Chuck Murdock who is on a Little League team in a small town in Montana. His father is a reserve fighter pilot who runs a lumberyard and has a friend who is a congressman. The congressman arranges a tour of a Minuteman missile silo for Chuck's class. The tour has an impact on Chuck, and Chuck decides he is going to give up the best thing in his life until there are no more nuclear weapons. Chuck quits Little League, even though he is a star pitcher and player.

Amazing Grace is a star basketball player for the Boston Celtics. He sees a small newspaper article about Chuck that catches his attention. He decides to meet Chuck; then he joins him and quits basketball. This begins a movement that thrusts Chuck into the center of national and world attention as athletes around the world join in.

Chuck chooses to stay his course through a multitude of events and people who try desperately to stop him. There are so many struggles with the value systems and people around Chuck that the film is a great source to examine values and paradigms. The issues become intriguing and a great source for dialogue.

If you choose to watch the movie, try to identify when Chuck's father has a paradigm shift. Does Chuck have more than one paradigm shift? What happens to the value systems of the primary characters? Who is the leader, and how do they influence others?

The unfortunate part is that once you start looking for these kinds of things in movies, it gives you a whole new perspective on watching movies and may change their entertainment value for you. In any event, you will not watch movies the same way after dissecting them for values, paradigms, and the leadership traits that we will explore.

Adult Learning

Since we are talking about learning by viewing case studies, we should discuss some learning issues. While a significant emotional event (SEE) will definitely produce some learning, we really want to try to avoid those events as they can become painful and embarrassing. The traditional thinking with respect to teaching supports repetition and memorization. The idea of segmented teaching insists that we finish a topic, and then move to another. This book is designed according to a totally different model of experiential learning or an adult learning model.

Professor and educational theorist David Kolb developed his adult/experiential learning model in 1981.[20] He describes four different methods in which adults learn:

1. Concrete experience: learning by feeling, going through specific experiences, relating to other people, and being sensitive to people and feelings.
2. Reflective observation: learning by watching, carefully observing, viewing from different perspectives, and looking for the meaning of things.
3. Abstract conceptualization: learning by thinking, logically analyzing ideas, systematic planning, and acting on an intellectual understanding of a situation.
4. Active experimentation: learning by doing, risk taking, and influencing people and events through action.

---

[20] Kolb, David A., *Experiential Learning*, Adult Learning Model, (New Jersey: Prentice Hall, 1981). The model was revised in 1986.

Kolb said that each person has no single method of learning but usually learns by a combination of methods. You may have a preferred method or style and may switch styles depending upon the situation or material.

Kolb's Learning Styles Inventory (LSI) can help you identify your preferred method of learning; however, we should remember that these "rat doctor" tests are not things that truly define us in all things or all situations. Frankl reminds us that we have choices; we can choose our response to a situation. What the LSI may do for us, though, is show us our general preference or show us that others have different preferences that we as leaders must understand and consider in all our actions. You can find Kolb's Learning Styles Inventory online and may want to take a few minutes to determine your preferred learning style.

Kolb divides the learning styles into four basic types:

- Accommodator
- Diverger
- Converger
- Assimilator

Kolb says that the *accommodator* style combines the learning steps of concrete experience with active experimentation. He says people in this style learn from hands-on experience. He says that this is important in action-oriented fields. The *diverger* combines concrete experience with reflective observation. People in this style tend to view a concrete experience from different perspectives and tend to observe rather than act. He says this style is good for arts, entertainment, and service careers. The *converger* combines abstract conceptualization and active experimentation. People in this area are good at making practical uses of things. These folks may like technical tasks rather than interpersonal or social problems.

The *assimilator* is a combination of abstract conceptualization and reflective observation. These folks may like to view large amounts of information and put it into some logical, concise order. They seem to be focused on the theory rather than practical use. They tend to be focused toward information and science.

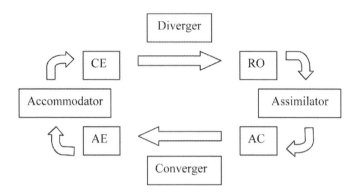

Example of Kolb's Learning Circle Model

So what does this have to do with learning leadership? If a converger is learning about a pen, he will get it very quickly, figure out how to use it, and be done. He is off to the next topic or going out to grab a beer and dinner. The assimilator says, "Not so fast! How does that work and why? What can we use it for, and how can we make it better?" The accommodator will be writing on the walls, and the diverger will be wondering about the philosophy behind the pen.

The point to all this is that people learn in different styles at different rates. For example, if we are discussing paradigms, the converger and the accommodator may be done with that topic while the diverger and the assimilator are still working through their thoughts about something we said five minutes ago, trying to make it fit into the events transpiring at the time.

To aid in the opportunity to learn, it is necessary to cover topics and concepts using several different methods. Some people will get a concept and move on while others want to think it over further. As a leader it is your job to keep things relevant and keep everyone involved by helping to bring out the thoughts of folks who are exploring more deeply than others.

Leaders need to know that some really good ideas or suggestions can be lost, along with the people giving them, if the leader moves too fast or too slow. The leader must pay attention and recognize what is going on with everyone on the team. A good leader will make sure he or she doesn't leave people behind and will offer everyone the opportunity to be involved.

Learning consists of more than reading, listening to lectures, and watching PowerPoint presentations. We have all heard the term *aha moments*, but do you really understand what that means? The concept, as I am using it here, comes from Kolb's theory of grasping and transforming. It refers to the ability to grasp the information being presented and transform it into an understanding using the process described above. It is the way we process information as adults: *Aha! I see how I can use this. I understand how this applies to what I want to do.* It is not merely learning a new skill, but learning how and when to apply that knowledge in multidimensional areas.

In police work, we teach the technical aspects of how to use a gun. We must also teach when to use the gun, when not to use the gun, and how to think while using the gun. That means we are going to have to visit all the learning styles and get past the grasping stage to the transforming stage of learning.

What is it that gets in the way of us grasping and transforming information in our brains? In getting information into our brains and into our long-term memories, we need to get it past our filters. We have filters that can block out information before it gets into the long-term memory and we are able to transform it into an aha moment.

We have been discussing paradigms and value systems and how they have an effect on the way we see the world. It is these things that filter information and prevent us from seeing what is right in front of us. These filters, made up of our past experiences, biases, prejudices, values, perceptions of the importance of the information, instructors, and so on, all have an effect on what gets absorbed.

To get past those filters, we must see a need for the information and develop a desire, curiosity, or some understanding of its importance. The teacher telling you something is necessary or important does not necessarily ensure that it will get through the filters. Sometimes we must break down the filters ourselves by trying to see why something is important to know. To do that, we must do some self-searching to figure out what biases, prejudices, or values we are dealing with. That means being very open and honest with ourselves, breaking down our barriers, and being open to others' points of view on our biases, prejudices, and values, which can be really scary! Others can help us identify those filters if we have the courage to allow that.

Who does not look forward to another PowerPoint presentation with handouts on the current sexual harassment policy? How about a class on ethics presented in a similar manner? If the material is not presented in a way that makes it interesting, many of us will probably filter out most of the information while playing Angry Birds on our iPhones.

We can refuse to listen because of the way someone looks, because of what we have heard about him or her, or even just because of the person's mannerisms. We tune out stuff all the time. This could be as simple as listening to the radio while driving and not realizing we missed the exit, or being bored at the staff meeting and missing some important due date for an assignment. We let those filters come and go as they please with very little control. If we are going to learn about ourselves and try to learn about leadership, we are going to have to acknowledge, identify, recognize, and control those filters.

But How Do I Learn?
Whose responsibility is learning? Is it correct to say that if the student has not learned, then the instructor did not teach correctly? Drucker said that it is absurd to think the organization is responsible for the development of its employees. According to Drucker, all development is self-development. Exactly how does the teacher take responsibility for the student's learning? Who chooses to learn or not to learn? If the material is available to read and research, then it is available for anyone to study, learn, and prepare.

The books and material we used in our course were well known and available to everyone. The reading list was always there, but nearly none of the participants had read any of it before being accepted to the course. After being allowed (upon their own requests) to attend the course on company time, many wanted to be paid overtime to read the material. Is it the responsibility of the organization to develop you to be a leader, or is it your choice to learn? Is it in the company's best interest to conduct leadership training? Most certainly there is a relationship between teaching and learning, but the responsibility lies with whom?

Do you think one student who desires to learn can overpower the teacher and empower the class to learn despite the shortcomings of the teacher? Can a great teacher overpower the lack of desire and motivation of a poor class? Can an individual in a poor class choose to learn and excel despite poor conditions? I believe there must be a shared responsibility between the student and the teacher, as partners in learning, to work together to create the environment for a great learning experience.

The teacher must care, prepare, motivate, maintain accountability, explain the purpose, communicate the vision, and be technically competent. Just as the leader is supposed to make learning a shared responsibility with the team, the student must take advantage of the opportunity to make it a shared experience.

Is the right question more important than the right answer? This seems like a silly question if you assume there is a right answer to any question. Some things vary so much with certain circumstances that we need to know the process to come to an answer rather than assuming there is a one-size-fits-all correct answer. Asking the right question may provide you with a number of useful possible answers. Sometimes it is the language that gets in the way of the understanding. I might not understand your question and may respond in a way that results in a misunderstanding and misinformation. Words are how we communicate our thoughts, but they can easily be misunderstood.

Humility is the key to learning. Humility is not weakness; it is strength. Through humility we are open to new ideas, open to the chance we are wrong in our assumptions, open to the idea that others know more and we can learn. Humility makes us approachable as leaders and encourages relationships with followers.

Knowledge is the greatest barrier to learning. It is not what I don't know that hurts me; it is what I think I know that ain't so! I worked with a guy who would throw a quarter out on the floor in the classroom and then say, "That is what I think I know; the rest of the room is what I don't know that I don't know." If I think I know it, I certainly can't learn it from you, and you can't teach me. It is wrong for a teacher to think he or she can teach you, enlighten you, or turn the lights on for you and make you understand, but it is not wrong for the teacher to try.

Teaching as a Subversive Activity[21] by Neil Postman is a great book to read if you are going to try to teach anything. Postman says that a good teacher rarely tells students what he or she thinks, refuses to accept one answer to a question, encourages student-to-student interaction as opposed to student-to-teacher interaction, and rarely summarizes, as it tends to bring closure and end further thought. He talks about placing yourself in the other person's perspective and arguing the other point of view in order to understand the issues. Dr. Covey makes the same point another way in his discussion of habit 5: *Seek first to understand and then to be understood.*[22]

You will see a lot of that in this book. There will not be closure on the subjects, but they will be left open so that we can come back to them to learn how they relate to the other concepts of leadership.

I usually end each class with the movie *Mr. Holland's Opus*,[23] which offers a great example of leadership. I love the part where high school music teacher

---

[21] Postman, Neil, and Weingartner, Charles, *Teaching as a Subversive Activity* (New York: Dell Publishing, 1969).

[22] Covey, Dr. Stephen R., *The 7 Habits of Highly Effective People* (New York: Simon and Shuster, 1989).

[23] *Mr. Holland's Opus*, Hollywood Pictures, 1995.

Mr. Holland finally realizes he is not reaching the students and tries a new approach that finally gets to them. He comes home so excited that the kids are participating, asking questions, and getting excited about learning, and all this happens when he stops trying to teach and begins to share as a part of the class. The students suddenly become a part of the process, and real learning occurs. Mr. Holland does not become wealthy as a high school music teacher, but he becomes rich in success, respect, and love.

Professor Sam Crowell writes in *A New Way of Thinking*,[24] "The greatest challenge facing education is not technology, not resources, not accountability—it is the need to discover with our students a new way of thinking ... viewing the world." He quotes Alfred North Whitehead, Thomas Kuhn, and Peter Drucker to support his views of looking at the whole rather than the parts. Peter Drucker said, "The fact that we are shifting from a Cartesian view of the universe, in which the accent has been on the parts and elements, to a configurations view, with emphasis on wholes and patterns, challenges every single dividing line between areas of study and knowledge."[25] (His article is worth reading to understand the different method of teaching and learning that this program represents.)

Plato said that the only true ignorance is arrogance. I loved facilitating the section of the course in which we discussed this point. I would always ask if anyone had ever read Plato. Most of the time, I got nothing but blank faces. Occasionally someone said they had read some of his work and knew who Socrates was; a few claimed to have drunk hemlock at some point in time. What I waited for was the guy who would always come back with "Why would we want to do that? Who cares?" Since Plato and other philosophers of his period are often considered the center of Western thought, I would ask why the skeptic was not interested in the origins of our thinking, the split between art and science, the differences in Eastern and Western philosophy, and so on. A frequent reply was, "We don't need to know—we get it through osmosis," to which I would say, "Thank you for making the point!"

---

[24] Crowell, Sam, "A New Way of Thinking: The Challenge for the Future," *Educational Leadership*, September 1989,
[25] Drucker, Peter, *The Age of Discontinuity* (New York: Harper and Row, 1969).

I had many top police executive officers come to graduations and thank me for working with their people and changing them. I would always tell them that it wasn't me that made changes; it was the students working on their own lives. The executives would praise the course, and we would discuss some of it. I would invite them to come down and sit in on a session since almost none of them had ever attended and the outline did not even begin to explain the material. Most of the time the reply was, "Thanks, but I know what it is." Maybe they did, but I have to also thank them for making my point: the only true ignorance is arrogance. A simple lack of knowledge is not ignorance, but no one can teach you if you think you already know.

What can we learn from Socrates, Plato, Aristotle, and an examination of Eastern versus Western thinking? I said management is a science, but leadership truly seems to be a combination of the art and science to be successful. While we can dissect it into parts and study it, we cannot use it if we don't view it as a whole.

In Eastern thinking, people look at the whole, not the parts. The Eastern approach to medicine is to cure the whole body. In Western thinking (reflected by the work of Aristotle and reductionism, for example), we tend to dissect everything into parts; we teach in segments, looking at the individual pieces, instead of taking in the whole picture (as with Plato or the holistic views in philosophy). This is something we should strive to do in this study of leadership; to keep our focus on the whole and on the parts.

As we look at the components of leadership, we will see that we cannot take out any of the leadership components and still have a good leader. A leader needs to be made up of all the components. Sound too perfect or too difficult? We are going to look into ways to make that possible. We will continually come back through the concepts as we review other concepts to try to keep in mind the whole picture of the leadership model.

Time to Get Involved
This is where things may start getting a little uncomfortable. This is an opportunity to become more involved in your own learning process. We can begin to examine some of these areas of behavior discussed and

identify our values, paradigms, filters, and barriers to learning. This can be a real-life experience of Kolb's experiential learning model. It is something you can experience, not just read or see in a PowerPoint presentation. It is your responsibility to learn, take a chance to experience something new, and take a step out of your comfort zone. It is your chance to demonstrate to yourself humility and a willingness to learn.

I want to visit lifetime goals and expectations and ask for some sharing of ideas. This way we begin to see how the areas of influence and concern, proactivity and reactivity, and paradigms really affect our lives.

Many programs use a lifetime goal-setting exercise of some type. The first time I experienced this was in a police-pilot training course after I was made manager of the helicopter unit. The course was designed to prepare for the worst possible tragedy and get us thinking about things we did not normally want to discuss. In flying, death or tragedy is only a breath away. The worst thing you can do is leave your family unprepared to handle a devastating event. We took a look at our long-term goals and made plans to prepare for the worst.

In this goal-setting exercise I want you to look at long-term versus short-term goals and how your area of influence applies to them. Identify and list the things that you want to accomplish in the long term. Then also list what you are doing in the short term to bring about or achieve those long-term goals. Please take a few minutes to complete this exercise before you continue, even if you have done this before. At the end of this chapter you will find a page to write down your goals.

Many people list financial or organizational success as goals. Some list promotion or higher positions in their companies as goals. I want you to think about how much control you have over those things. Consider, for example, the goal of being hired or promoted to a particular position. You don't have control over the other people who are applying for the job, but you do have control over your own education and preparation for the position. You have control over your preparation for the interview. You can choose to improve your interpersonal relationships. You have some control over your health, over how much you exercise and what you eat (but maybe not over some disease you may encounter). You have control over what you wear and your general appearance. All of these things may have an effect on the choice the decision makers come to regarding who will receive the job or promotion, or their choice may simply boil down to selecting the candidate whom they believe shares their values, as in our selection-process exercise.

Success may be on your list too, but many people have very different views of success. If someone in the company is successful in climbing to the top of the division by stepping on the backs of others, are they successful? Do you need to be respected to have a successful career? If a person has done a poor job for forty years, but made it to retirement in the same position he or she started in, is that person successful? I suppose we may have some difficulty in defining success and may need to revisit this. Frankl says that you cannot pursue success; success *ensues*. According to him we need to find meaning for our lives, some work or purpose, and we must constantly strive for a worthwhile goal.[26]

Look at the goals you listed. Now consider if you had just been told you have only six months left to live. Would any of those long-term or lifetime goals change? Would that help you to focus on what is important in your life? This does not only apply to police officers, pilots, or people with terminal diseases but to everyone. No one going to work on 9/11 expected a tragedy that day. One must realize that there is the possibility in everyone's life that things can end unexpectedly. Take some time to think about this. Did your goals change? Are you focused on what is important?

Many people's goals involve leaving their families financially secure. That seems like something we would all want to consider, but is it equally important to leave your children with good values, morals, and ethics, and healthy minds and lifestyles? I want to leave mine with the knowledge and ability to live life to the fullest, grow on their own, and create their own financial security.

---

[26] Frankl, Viktor E., *Man's Search for Meaning*, 12–13, 78, 110.

Looking at your long-term plans and figuring out how to work toward them with your short-term goals is an essential part of looking at yourself and getting your house in order before you start trying to lead. Followers want to look up to you, but if your personal life is a disaster, they would be foolish to follow your lead.

I have seen many emotions come out as people begin to look at their inner selves and see things they don't really care for. We all have demons of some type that we want to shed. The question is, *are you really willing to look?*

This is why understanding dialogue is so important. Peter Senge tells us that "in dialogue people become observers of their own thinking."[27] This should sound like another important quality that our best leaders possess, the ability to be open in seeking advice and providing feedback. A good leader is going to put aside their ideas and assumptions and truly seek the best option. Senge further explains that "through dialogue people can help each other to become aware of the incoherence in each other's thoughts and in this way collective thoughts become more and more coherent."[28] Others can help us see ourselves more clearly.

Think about the goals you have listed and what factors are hindering you from pursuing those goals. List the things that are hindering you and the things that are supporting your pursuit of those goals. Look for ways to change the things that are stopping you from progressing and ways to enhance the things that are helping you reach the goals you have identified.

In the first couple of chapters I would like you to look inwardly and try to be honest with yourself. Socrates said the unexamined life is not worth living, because he believed that the purpose of life was spiritual and personal growth. Personal growth in leadership is our goal.

Have you thought about these things before? Are you open to criticism and to other perspectives and ideas? Do you engage in dialogue to solve

---

[27] Senge, Peter M., *The Fifth Discipline: The Art and Practice of the Learning Organization* (New York: Doubleday, 1990), 242.
[28] Ibid., 243.

problems? Are you in control of your responses? Are you keeping focused on your long-term goals and operating in your area of influence? Do you act the same at home and at work? Is your value system intact? How do others view you? What would they say at your retirement or your funeral? Do you really care about others, or are you selfish? Do you present and represent the things you listed as skills, traits, and values of the best leaders?

Review and Evaluation

Every day you will be involved with events like the ones we have discussed in this chapter. In the course, we asked students to keep a journal and make entries about some of the concepts we discussed. I think it is a good thing to keep some kind of log or make some notes about how you see the concepts play out in your life, whether they involve work or your personal time.

The concept of leadership is something that is value driven, and we do not leave those values at home or at work (I think we refer to those people with multiple personalities as needing professional help!). So, I am leaving room for you to make some notes at the end of each chapter and suggesting some concepts to review and log. If something that we have discussed strikes you in a meaningful way, make a note, discuss it with someone, and get another person's thoughts on the subject.

In this chapter we want to review our paradigms. Completing the goal-setting exercise in which you list lifetime goals will help you identify your values. Watch yourself in day-to-day activities to see if those values are consistent or whether they change with certain events or decisions. When you make choices, which values come into play? Are you making choices based on a utilitarian, moral rights, or justice model? Do your choices match your values? What caused you to make a particular choice or reject an idea? Was this fair?

Are you looking at things with a long-term perspective? What events transpired to help you choose to look at the end results instead of the short-term advantage?

Notes

Lifetime Goal Setting

Long-term goals:

Short-term goals:

SELECTION PROCESS

As the training manager for the HR division, you must select an employee to fill a temporary six-month training assignment in a specialized advertising unit. This is a rare opportunity that is highly sought after. All of the employees listed below are qualified and have requested the assignment. Choose the candidate that you would select and be prepared to articulate the basis for your selection.

1. John is an experienced employee who presently handles similar assignments in his division. This training would enhance his effectiveness and subsequently benefit the company's overall efficiency and effectiveness.

2. Susan is a newer employee. She is sharp, bright, and experienced. The CEO has encouraged affirmative action decisions, as women are a definite minority in highly advanced positions. This has become an issue with the local press and the surrounding community. Based on her past outstanding performance, she is deserving of a reward.

3. Tom is an outstanding employee with a tremendous record and experience at the company, but very little advertising exposure. He has applied for a permanent advertising position, and this training assignment would greatly enhance his chances of being chosen for a permanent assignment.

Your selection:

Chapter Two

Breaking through the Barriers

If you watched the movie *Amazing Grace and Chuck* and tried to dissect the values and paradigm shifts, you may have found it difficult or confusing. That is pretty much par for the course. So let me try to add to the confusion and give you my take on the paradigm change for Chuck's father, Mr. Murdock.

Mr. Murdock thinks he has his paradigm and his values in line. After all, he is a fighter pilot, prepared to give his life in defense of his country. He does not understand that Chuck also wants to defend his country and protect the lives of his family members. Chuck believes the best way to do that is by eliminating all nuclear weapons.

A large fight involving the athletes and the townsfolk erupts on the front lawn of the Murdocks' home. Afterward, Amazing Grace and Chuck's father go to the backyard to play one-on-one basketball. During some rough play and an exchange of barbs, Amazing says that he is "jealous as hell" (referring to Chuck's father and his family). Dad finally gets it. He finally sees just how Chuck's method of protecting his country is better than his own and how fortunate he is to have a son like Chuck. Dad's values get rearranged to fall in line with Chuck's paradigm, but this creates a new set of loyalty conflicts for Dad.

Take some time to watch the movie. You may enjoy it, and it will help you to understand the concepts better.

Learning Humility

In the course we continued to review value systems with the book *Jonathan Livingston Seagull*[29] to enhance our understanding of values and how they make us what we are. *JLS* was the third book used as background for the course.

In this book, Jonathan is a young bird frustrated with the routine of the flock. To avoid the status quo he sets out to improve his own ability to fly, dive, and gather food. He is quite successful at improving his abilities, but also a bit reckless, and he endangers the other birds. The elders of the flock have warned Jonathan before and are upset by this. Jonathan is called front and center to a meeting where he expects to be rewarded. Instead, he is expelled from the flock.

After some time, Jonathan meets other gulls who were also on their own and have formed a flock. Jonathan is mentored by other gulls, including Chiang, and learns much as he transcends to a new level. Eventually Jon feels a need to return to his old flock. Jonathan is still an outcast, but he has developed a new attitude and level of thinking that is noticed by others. Jonathan must stay outside the flock, but begins to have a significant following as the others in the flock recognize new qualities of humility and caring in him.

We look at this story for a number of reasons. We want to examine our values as they compare to Jonathan's. We want to see what happened to Jonathan on his journey and the process that transformed him. We want to know how to deal with Jonathans as leaders.

We can all be Jonathans at times, recklessly running about in an organization and causing havoc as we strive to make things better and show everyone just how good we are. When we do that, a number of things happen. People start to notice us in both a good and bad light. Some folks may be influenced to follow along, but others may see us as a threat to their progress and the organization as a whole. If we are challenging

---

[29] Bach, Richard, *Jonathan Livingston Seagull* (New York: Avon Books, 1970).

the organizational values as Jonathan did with the flock, we can easily be ostracized from the group.

Conformity to the organization's values is preferred in most businesses. Sometimes innovators are rewarded, even if they are reckless. Some people just seem to get breaks and rise quickly; sometimes those same people end up in court trying to explain their reckless behavior. What we need to understand is that the organization is made up of people who set the organizational values. Those people are always looking to see if your values match the organization's values and theirs (think about the selection process).

Humility is not the same as weakness. Striving to be noticed or to gain recognition or success is not a quality we look for in leaders. To obtain success or become "a prince by villainy or other means"[30] will not endear you to the masses. To become a leader in the organization you will need to earn the respect of the followers. Leaders cannot demand followers. People willingly follow leaders. Managers may lead through fear or position; leaders do not.

Jonathan has time to learn while he is an outcast. Chiang takes Jonathan under his wing and teaches him about humility and about having the caring developer mind-set. Leaders share values with the people who follow, but this must be something that is observed and admired by their followers. You cannot just tell people you have certain values; you must demonstrate them.

You may simplify this by calling it "leading by example," but it tends to be more complex than that. This is why you must examine your values, define them, and share them with others through your deeds, words, and actions. This involves living your values on and off the job. There is no way to turn those value systems on and off, if they are truly a part of you. You know the person you are all the time. Don't think you can fool everyone.

Leaders need to recognize that Jonathans can be risky but have tremendous potential in organizations. The leader's job is to direct that energy into

---

[30] Machiavelli, *The Prince*.

productive areas, not to squash it. Jonathans need someone to help identify the values that are important and prioritize them so they can be productive members of the organization. Risk taking can be an important element of leadership. Admiral Stockdale, the top commander of our POWs in North Vietnam during the Vietnam War, took tremendous risks by setting up a chain of command and an officer's code of conduct during their period of captivity. He demonstrated his commitment and humility by maintaining an atmosphere of forgiveness and compassion for those who broke during torture and interrogation. Living these concepts will help you move on just as they helped Jonathan.

Jonathan did offer a positive change for the organization that improved production and quality of life for everyone, but he needed to get over his personal desire for recognition. A leader's motivation is recognized by his or her followers. Jonathan as a young bird wanted to be the one to show the way. He expected rewards and recognition for showing everyone how to better themselves.

There is something about this that is problematic. If I come to tell you I can make you better, I will probably be met with a defensive posture. You may think, "Who does he think he is telling me I am wrong and he can make me better?" However, if you observe me day after day doing something more productive than what you're doing, you may come and ask for advice. You are then open to suggestion and are not defensive.

If your motivation is only to help and not to stand there waving a flag for recognition, people may be more receptive to you. Frankl explains that the more one forgets himself by giving himself to a cause to help another person, the more human he is and the more he actualizes himself.[31] All of this seems to point to the quality of humility being an essential part of the leader.

Jonathans are a very necessary part of our organizations. It is not a new concept in leadership to use energetic new people with better ideas. Debra

---

[31] Frankl, Viktor E., *Man's Search for Meaning*, 115.

Meyerson of Stanford University's School of Engineering and Graduate School of Business refers to Jonathans as *tempered radicals*. [32] This is a reference to people who are radical, but want to succeed within the organization. It is the leader's job to engage these "radicals" and temper their approach so that it fits within the organizational values and works with the veterans (the "flock") to precipitate change and improve the organization.

Monika Byrd wrote about this same concept in her Phi Theta Kappa 2005 Leadership Brief, *The Roles of Veterans and Radicals in Organizational Change*.[33] She noted that leaders need to be able to integrate new technology, as well as new people with bold ideas for change, into the organization. Leaders enhance the understanding of all parties to the values at work within the organization and help them understand humility and patience so they don't get expelled from the flock.

What'd I Say?

To communicate our values to others we use a variety of methods. One is that we talk. Our words can be interpreted in many different ways because it is not just *what* we say, but how we say it. You can send an e-mail with a certain intent that is completely misinterpreted on the other end. We can make a statement sound like a question. We can say words but clearly indicate we don't mean them or do not want to do what we are articulating. It doesn't take much to create doubt and misunderstanding if we want to.

Something as simple as a wink, gesture, pause, change in tone, voice fluctuation, eye movement, raised eyebrow, curled lip, smile, or laugh can change the meaning of the words. Communication is mostly perceived through our body language, not our words. We need to be aware of the whole message we are sending, not just the verbal part.

---

[32] Meyerson, Debra, *Tempered Radicals: How People Use Difference to Inspire Change at Work*, a Stanford University Graduate School of Business Executive Briefing Film (Mill Valley, CA: Cantola Productions, 2001).

[33] Byrd, Monika, Phi Theta Kappa, http://www.ptk.org/leaddev/news/item116.htm, March 2005.

I can tell everyone in the staff meeting that upper management wants us to follow a new policy, but if I speak in a certain tone, roll my eyes, drop the memo in front of me, and stare at the staff, what message will I send? It is very easy to let people know you do not support policies, goals, or objectives without putting that sentiment into words. Those messages can also be transferred without us trying. If we don't agree or support the message, people are going to see what we are thinking through our body language.

This is an incongruent value communication; when we say one thing but mean something different. In class we watched a short video called "The Constitution, that Delicate Balance" to study some of these actions.[34] It is an excellent study in incongruent value communications. In this video we get to see attorneys, judges, journalists, civil rights advocates, district attorneys, politicians, and others all speaking about their value systems.

The scenario is a facilitated discussion about the rights of criminal defendants to a fair trial. Although they think they are talking about justice, they are really telling us about their own values. We get to see them lay out the values that make them who they are, and we receive insights into what they really think, despite the words that keep coming out. Everyone is arguing for their own perspectives or on behalf of the course of action that will benefit them the most. It becomes clear they could really care less about a defendant's right to a fair trial or justice.

One defense attorney says he thinks the defendant is scum, but being offered $100,000 to take his case is "starting to make a pretty nice fellow out of this guy." Another says that he firmly believes that the defendant has a right to a fair trial without the $100,000 fee, but this lawyer is also influenced by the fact that he has "a daughter in college." Yet another says whether he took the case would depend on whether or not it was an election year.

In one scene a judge is questioned regarding the admissibility of a confession obtained without a Miranda warning. She responds that if the

---

[34] *The Constitution, That Delicate Balance,* Episode 4, "Criminal Justice and a Defendant's Right to a Fair Trial" PBS, 1984.

officers were encouraged to remember well (at which point she pauses, smirks, tilts her head and chuckles) and they still said the confession came without warning, she would be forced to dismiss it. Most of the class thought that her body language indicated she wanted the officers to lie and make the confession admissible, but that is not what her words said.

We see it every day, and we do it every day. What we must begin to do is understand the effect it has on us as leaders. If we are not conveying our honest values to our followers they will pick up on it. If you lie to your people they will not trust you, and trust is an essential element of leadership.

Loyalty Conflicts

We find ourselves in value conflicts all the time. Imagine that your organization or boss wants you to do something in a way you are not comfortable with. If you are not comfortable with it, the reason may be that there is some value conflict. If honesty and truth are important to you and the boss wants you to fudge some numbers, you will have a conflict and need to make a choice. What will you do when someone asks you, "Where do your loyalties lie?"

I don't know if loyalty is an important or desirable quality in leadership, so we need to explore it. You might expect loyalty from the people you lead; you might expect loyalty from the people whom you follow, and they may expect it from you. You certainly expect loyalty from your friends, your family, and your spouse. Are you loyal to your country, loyal to your religion, and loyal to your company too? So what exactly is loyalty, and what or whom should we be loyal to? There are so many things that seem to want your loyalty, but what really deserves your unwavering faith or support?

Most definitions involve being faithful to a person, cause, institution, or government, or some other form of fidelity. That would seem consistent with the thought of unwavering faith or support. Some people demand loyalty. Your spouse and family expect loyalty, but how about if they commit a crime? Are you expected to cover for them and remain loyal, or is it loyal to turn them in? You may be loyal to your boss, but what if he or she is falsifying reports? You are expected to be loyal to your company, but if it is failing and going under, are you going down with the ship? What would it take for you to quit your company?

Robert E. Lee, a Confederate general during the Civil War, chose to be loyal to his home state of Virginia, even though he had sworn an oath to the United States of America. He chose to fight against the country he had sworn to protect through a multitude of loyalty conflicts. Would you ever consider not being loyal to your country? Is this an issue of loyalty or patriotism? I think we are supposed to share the values of freedom and independence as a nation. If the government clearly departed from our value system, what would you do?

In the Rampart Division at LAPD during the late 1990s some officers were so loyal to each other and certain leaders that they committed criminal acts together. They also falsified arrests and reports, knowing full well the consequences of these actions. Many years earlier in the Hollywood Division, a group of officers showed loyalty to each other and committed burglaries while on duty. They later sold the stolen property to other officers who kept quiet about the illegal acts.

Television news program *60 Minutes* did a piece on cheating at the Naval Academy called "A Matter of Honor."[35] The story described how midshipmen had cheated on an exam. One person came forward and admitted he had seen the exam prior to the test. The Academy wanted to know who else had seen it, but he did not want to say. No one else was willing to come forward, break their loyalty to the others, and identify the conspirators. Eventually, four admitted cheating and were expelled. The investigation indicated hundreds had been involved but could not prove it.

Is it ever a good thing to be loyal to a person or a group? When does that loyalty start and end? What is it that you should be loyal to?

I think we should expect to be loyal to values and to people who share those values. If a person or a group deviates from those shared values, then

---

[35] *60 Minutes*, "A Matter of Honor," CBS 1992.

that loyalty will end. I feel we all have a responsibility to speak up when someone is violating values that we share so that we can keep them from stepping into areas where they should not go. People need to understand there is no friendship beyond that point; if they go there, you are not going with them. Maybe that is what true loyalty is, being courageous enough to step up and stop a friend, a spouse, a family member, a coworker, a boss, or others from making wrong judgments or actions that will impact them forever.

The movie *Twelve O'Clock High*[36] has been used in many management and leadership programs, including ours. It is a great tool to look at the components of leadership. In the film, General Savage says, "Loyalty is a fine thing," but this may be an incongruent value communication at the place and time he says it. He may be realizing that loyalty might be at the root of the group's problems and is not as fine a thing as he once thought. He may be experiencing a paradigm change on the subject of loyalty.

In the movie, the members of the 918th Bomb Wing are very loyal to the commander, Colonel Keith Davenport, despite sustaining many casualties with him in command. What is it about the concept of loyalty that could make them feel so committed to a person that they would risk their lives in support of him?

We will look at this concept in more detail in the next few pages and in other portions of the book as we further examine leadership traits and values. Issues involved in this are not only loyalty but also courage, supportive confrontation, ethics, values, principles, and power. These are tough leadership concepts to embrace because they could result in you having to choose a different path than the ones your friends, your job, and maybe your family would choose for you. It is always easy to *say* that you will be true to yourself and your values, but living that may be a bit more difficult. Loyalty is a good thing to have, but it is easy to lose if you abuse it, and it has a direct relationship to power and trust.

---

[36] *Twelve O'Clock High*, Twentieth Century Fox Pictures, 1949.

We looked at this film from a different perspective than those I have seen in other programs. We have already talked a bit about accountability and responsibility, so now let's look at Theory X and Theory Y, developed by management professor Doug McGregor, as they are demonstrated in the movie.

Theory X and Theory Y

In 1955, Doug McGregor wrote the *Human Side of Enterprise*,[37] in which he introduced his Theory X and Theory Y concepts. Management professors and authors Paul Hersey and Ken Blanchard produced something similar with their situational leadership[38] models. It appears to me their work is based on the x/y axis of McGregor's work. Many folks have produced other similar examples.

The basic approach is that Theory X people don't want to work and need to be managed, driven, watched over, and given explicit directions and simple tasks. They are basically task driven. Theory Y people want to work; they are self-motivated and trustworthy and need little supervision—just get out of the way and let them do their work. They are people types. So the model evolved into a consideration of task management versus people management.

My colleague, Lieutenant Cunningham, told me he felt a lot of the situational leadership stuff was just BS. He would say that you can't be a leader without a task; you can't be a leader without change. According to him, a people person gets 100 percent of nothing done; you kick them in the butt to stop mistakes because you love them and believe in them; then get out of the way and let them do it. As they progress, you give more freedom, responsibility, authority, but never back off the accountability for the task.

That statement sounds like the whole situational leadership model by Hersey and Blanchard, just put a little more bluntly and concisely. I think

---

[37] McGregor, Doulas, *The Human Side of Enterprise* (New York: McGraw Hill, 1960).
[38] Hersey, Paul, and Blanchard, Ken, *Management of Organizational Behavior* (Englewood Cliffs, NJ: Prentice-Hall, 1982).

we see much of this in *Twelve O'Clock High* and in the style of General Savage.

The management style in X/Y theory seems to be frequently misunderstood. The movie *Twelve O'Clock High* can really help with seeing the difference. Colonel Davenport is a really nice, respected commander of the 918th Bomb Group, which is based in England during World War II. They are flying multiengine, propeller-driven, bomber aircraft (B-17s) on missions to attack Germany.

As the movie opens, Colonel Davenport is returning from a mission that resulted in the loss of five aircraft. Each plane contained ten men, so fifty men lost their lives. Many more men were wounded, and the other aircraft suffered substantial battle damage.

At headquarters, General Savage is working as the adjutant to the general managing the 918th, as well as several other groups or bomber wings. They are concerned about the losses suffered by the 918th and have a discussion about the problem. They decide it all boils down to a leadership issue, and they both head down to the 918th Bomb Group to investigate.

(I'd like to pause for a moment to make a note about the incredible courage that our soldiers displayed during WWII. A B-17 was a slow airplane, cruising at 182 knots (209 mph), with a service ceiling of 35,000 feet. It was an easy target if it was at low altitude, but flying at low altitudes, around 9,000 feet during the daytime, allowed for precision bombing of German submarine pens. Each plane carried ten men as a crew and only 8,000 pounds of bombs for short-range missions or a maximum of 4,000 pounds for long-range missions. So, for a long-range mission of 800 miles, each plane could take ten guys and four bombs, each a thousand pounds. The prevailing thought was that a crew's luck would run out in fifteen missions. Like I said, they showed incredible courage!)

Davenport really cares about his people. He is devastated at the loss of personnel, and he blames it on bad luck. As the commanding general questions him over the circumstances surrounding the loss, it becomes evident that a mistake in navigation put them over the target late and made them sitting ducks for the enemy. A navigator missed a checkpoint and caused the error.

Upon the discovery of the error, Savage offers more experienced navigators to replace this one, but Davenport refuses because he believes it will hurt his navigators' feelings and confidence. Davenport tells them that there isn't a man there who would not trust his navigator with his life. (Of course, the fact is that fifty of them did—and lost their lives because of it.) During the exchange, the commanding general identifies the problem and relieves Davenport of command, eventually replacing him with Savage. Savage is charged with getting the 918th on its feet and into sync with the other groups.

After Davenport is relieved of his duties, Savage returns to the group with a tough, hard-tailed wing-commander approach that is not welcome. He sets out on a mission to improve performance and make the group operate as a fine, cohesive unit—and he kicks some serious butt in the process!

During his initial briefing, Savage challenges everyone to get on board or transfer out. Everyone in the 918th Bomb Group is loyal to the country, the mission, and each other; however they are also loyal to Davenport. This results in the pilots sending Lieutenant Bishop (a valor nominee) in to see Savage and request transfers for all of them.

I pause the movie at this point and ask who in the film represents Theory X and who represents Theory Y. Who is the task-oriented manager, and who is the people guy? Most people see Davenport as the people guy and Savage as a tyrant just fixated on the task. Few people seem to notice that Davenport is a really wonderful guy *who is getting his people killed right and left*. The group loves Davenport. Because they are very loyal to him, they are very upset that he was relieved of his duty. Davenport loves his guys and is loyal to them also. After some short discussion we continue with the film.

Major Harvey Stovall is the executive officer's adjutant for the 918th Bomb Group in the film. Harvey quickly recognizes the loyalty issues with Savage and Davenport. He realizes what needs to be done, and where to place his loyalty. He tells Savage that his loyalties lie with the 918th and that he wants them to succeed. Together they delay transfers, which results in a visit from the inspector general to hear complaints.

As the movie goes on, we see Savage refusing to accept failures, training his men until they get it right, punishing those who are not performing, and rewarding those who do; he relentlessly pushes the 918th to perform as a team and to hold each other accountable. Davenport comes to visit Savage and tells him that he is pushing too hard—they are only boys. Savage's response is that they are not boys—they are men; Savage believes they are capable of doing this on their own. The group finally flies several very successful missions with virtually no losses.

Savage eventually lays out the importance of the mission and vision to Bishop, who begins to understand. Bishop steps up in the meeting with the inspector general, showing his leadership abilities in pulling the other pilots together.

We take another break from the movie here to discuss tasks and people again. Most participants start to see the difference at this point. Savage is the one who trusts his people; Davenport is the one who does not. Davenport steals the responsibility from the boys and tries to take it all on himself. He does not do it because of a lack of care—on the contrary, he does care—but he has lost sight of what his job is as the leader. Savage cares just as much as Davenport, but he understands his job and is willing to make the personal sacrifice necessary to develop his men.

By placing the responsibility where it belongs and holding people accountable, Savage develops a team in which everyone is accountable for the outcome; the pilots, the crews, the ground personnel, and everyone involved have total buy-in for the mission. They are flying missions now, and nearly everyone returns home safely. They enjoy a period during which camaraderie and performance are at their peak.

Savage now must fight off the groups' attempts to be loyal to him and keep them loyal to the mission, the country, and each other. Eventually it becomes time for Savage to step away and turn the group over to someone else who can command.

Leadership has some downfalls. (We will look at Machiavelli later on and discuss if it is better to be loved or feared as the leader.) The men of the 918th were operating out of a fear of Savage in the beginning, but there is no doubt that they love him in the end. He earned the respect, love, and admiration of everyone on the base, but he couldn't get that without loving them back. This is where value conflicts start to arise. Savage begins to privately worry about the people he loves, and as they fall victim to war, he has some deep conflicts with sending them on more missions that will result in some of their deaths. At the movie's end, Savage's conflicts eventually take their toll, causing him to suffer a mental breakdown.

This is something all leaders may experience at some point. The problem is that when we are not loyal to our own values it can have mental and physical effects on us, causing stress, ulcers, illness, nervous breakdowns, rage, and so on.

If you watch the movie, think about all the things we have discussed so far in the book. Every concept we have discussed and will discuss is in this movie in some form. Compare Davenport and Savage to yourself. Think about this in the context of your work setting and your family or personal settings. Savage and Davenport both display values of leadership. Which do you want to be like? Which man would you want to work for? Does it matter to your coworkers if you hold everyone accountable? Which leader would you put your trust in? Who deserves your loyalty? Who works better in the short term? The long term? Who has the respect? Which leader leaves the unit best able to function without him being present? Who is less selfish? Who is the developer?

There are so many questions we can explore with *Twelve O'Clock High*. Can you see how the right question is better than the right answer? It becomes difficult to choose what is right. In *Amazing Grace and Chuck*, Chuck asks Amazing, "How do you know what is right?" Amazing says that sometimes "there is no real way to tell, you just do what feels right at the moment." How do we choose the right path as a leader?

"Zen and the Art of Management"

"Zen and the Art of Management"[39] is a *Harvard Business Review* article (which is available online as are most of the articles referenced in this book) written by business consultant Richard Pascale; it compares Japanese-style management to American-style management.

Pascale discusses ambiguity as a tool in decision making and highlights the difference between choosing and deciding. He discusses the recognition of employees through "BLT" (bright lights and trumpets) and through implied recognition. He also talks about the dangers of being a mentor to one, as opposed to a leader for all. Let's take a closer look.

Ambiguity

In Western society, we view taking decisive action on issues as evidence of true leadership and might not view ambiguity as any form of leadership at all. We like people who can make decisions, cut out the multiple teams to evaluate possible solutions, and get things done. Pascale's article takes a couple of different turns in examining perceived differences in management styles. He discusses how employees can be manipulated when managers ask for their opinions, but then steer them toward an already predetermined course of action.

You may find the idea of using ambiguity in leadership a difficult concept to wrap your arms around. It may seem like the polar opposite of leadership, but what leader doesn't want input and buy-in from his or her teams? What leader can possibly think that leading by "my way or the highway" is going to command respect and love from those being led? Good leaders always ask for input. Good leaders always listen to the followers. If you as a leader want to build trust, respect and improve production, then you want to get the team on board with the vision of the company.

---

[39] Pascale, Richard Tanner, "Zen and the Art of Management," *Harvard Business Review*, March–April 1978.

So what use do we have for ambiguity? We want our people to have a voice in the management of the company. It makes them feel they are important to the task. It lets them own a part of the project, the company, and their work. To accomplish this, we need to allow them to have meaningful input. That means that we must simply give them the opportunity to participate *without manipulating the outcome.*

One student in my leadership program gave an example concerning his police chief, who wanted to proceed with a new team-policing concept. He asked the officers in his department to meet and give suggestions, ideas, and direction for the new course he wanted for the department. When the group asked him what this might look like, he said he had no idea, offering virtually no concept of a direction.

The team did proceed with research and generating ideas, and eventually they presented a plan. The chief rejected it; he said the plan was not what he was looking for or expecting from the group. To put it mildly, the group was really upset. They were mad that they had wasted time and been manipulated and lied to. Most members quit, either because they saw no point in continuing the effort or because they were so offended they refused to do it. A scenario like this one is not what I am suggesting for the use of ambiguity. As we get further into leadership concepts we will talk about vision and the way leaders convey vision to an organization and the ambiguity that exists in that process.

In his article, Pascale suggests that the manager gives the task to the employee groups, but keep a direction in mind. The manager should then guide them toward the conclusion he desires.

I believe a good leader explains the vision to the team but stays out of the way to allow them to move through a process. John F. Kennedy did this during the Cuban Missile Crisis by purposely being absent from brainstorming meetings. If you have a definite idea of where you want to go and what you get back is not what you expected, you have a problem. If you are not willing to settle for the result you get, then it might be better not to be too ambiguous. If people think they are being manipulated, they will not look at you as a leader.

In using ambiguity as a tool, it is important to avoid manipulation and provide guidance so that the team goes in the direction you want. You must also maintain an open mind that they may go somewhere you did not expect and produce a solution better than what you had hoped for.

Choosing versus Deciding

Pascale says that in American culture we like to announce things. We seem to have a need to be in charge and set the direction and tone. We like decisiveness; anything else is viewed as a weak approach. We consider decisiveness to be macho, masculine, or strong.

Is there a difference between choosing and deciding? A decision seems to refer to something that is final and that you own, as in "I have made the decision …" A decision implies finality and that the process is closed to other options. It also becomes personal; if this is "my decision," I tend to become defensive about it. In choice, there seems to be less ownership, less ego, less finality; it appears that other options may still be there. People may be more apt to provide other options if they feel you are open and receptive. Being approachable is a desirable quality for a leader.

There are times in emergency management when we must be decisive, but we are foolish if we rule out other perspectives and suggestions. My self-defense instructor in the police academy made one thing very clear, "If what you are doing is not working, try something else!"

We should always be open to options. We can really get ourselves or our organizations in trouble if we decide our path is the only path and then insist on sticking to it and ignoring all other input. I compare it to a SWAT operation: the SWAT commander may be strong and in command, but always has a contingency plan and never stops taking input and reviewing the course of action for options. The commander chooses an action, but is always open to change.

As I've explained, the only true ignorance is arrogance. This is true in any business. You must always watch for changes in the market that will affect the company and prepare to compensate for these changes.

Keeping this in mind, we can use ambiguity in this situation also. Simply saying, "I think this is the best course of action, but I am open to suggestions," might work wonders to aid in bringing about a successful outcome. Enlisting the aid of fellow employees will get the buy-in we are looking for and empower our employees.

Implied Recognition

A good manager or leader will reward team members for a job well done. Pascale calls it bright lights and trumpets; we might call it employee-of-the-month awards, employee recognition reports, atta boys, or atta girls. Pascale gets into something else with the Eastern thinking of implied recognition.

Of course there is benefit to the written expressions of appreciation, thank yous, and the recognition of employees in front of peers and management, but there is more. People like challenging assignments. They appreciate being trusted with bigger, more important tasks than they were entrusted with previously. They revel in being asked for their opinions and input on jobs above their pay grades. If they think the boss has trusted them with this very important task because they have shown the ability to perform, you can bet they are going to do their very best not to let the boss or the company down.

You can expect exceptional performance out of them if they are trying to please you and make both you and them look good. We will discuss these concepts further when we talk about power, authority, empowerment, trust, respect, vision, and focus.

A Leader to All

One more issue I'd like to look at from Pascale's article is the idea of being a mentor to one as opposed to a leader to all. Pascale discussed the problem of treating everyone as equal but not the same. What kinds of problems develop when you as a manager begin to single out certain employees that you wish to mentor? It can create issues of jealously, and unfair accusations from all the others who are not being mentored. This may occur even if others are not interested in seeking promotions or improving their performance.

Think back to the discussion of *Twelve O'Clock High* and consider the idea of mentorship and whether it can create loyalty issues. General Savage had consistent rules for everyone and made the same demands on everyone, but he did not treat everyone the same. While he had some special people he was mentoring for leadership positions within the group, he was a leader to all. Obviously, it is necessary to groom some folks for promotion, but it is essential to treat everyone as equal. You don't want to be everybody's friend; you do want to be everybody's leader. Leaders walk a fine line in this area, which we will discuss later.

Pascale's article aims to help leaders maintain a developer mind-set, which is essential to being a good leader. This mind-set, coupled with humility, made Jonathan Seagull successful when he returned to the flock.

Power Trips

The discussion of "Zen and the Art of Management" touched on empowering employees by getting them involved in their own management. The idea that we get power by giving power away is a foreign concept to some managers. Some people just want to have all the power and be in control of everything. We all hate those people and generally refer to them as micromanagers. A micromanager is in charge only because someone put them in charge, and they manage through fear and by the authority invested in them.

That is not how leaders operate. Leaders operate through power. Leaders get things done through other people who do those things because they want to. Leaders inspire and motivate people to get things done. Remember that people always have a choice. They can choose to tell you to pound sand and walk away at any time; yes, that may have consequences, but it is still a choice they have. Ultimately, you cannot force anyone to do anything they do not want to do if they are willing to suffer the consequences for refusing.

Blaine N. Lee talks about types of power in his book, *Power Principle, Influence with Honor.* [40] He divides power into three types: coercive, utility, and legitimate.

He claims that coercive power is based on what you can do *to* others as fear and punishment.

Utility power is based on what you can do *for* others as in request or reward. It can be dependent on rank or position in the organization; special skills and knowledge (expertise); your appeal or attractiveness (charisma); having information of value; opportunities (an emergency event); access to people, goods or commodities of value (resources); your ability to make things happen; or your ability to give feedback or appraisal to others.

Legitimate power is based on what you can do *with* others. Legitimate power is created when the group believes, trusts, respects, share goals, and willingly follows the leader.

This is a very short summary of Lee's description of different types of power for us to compare. We used a different method of interpreting power in class, dividing it into power verses authority, and how it is obtained or granted. I think Lee's description of coercive power and many of the utility power traits are authority, while legitimate power is a better definition of what power is.

---

[40] Types of power. Lee, Blaine N., *The Power Principle: Influence with Honor* (New York: Fireside, 1988).

Authority	**Power**
Positional	Nonpositional
Granted by the organization	Given by followers
Granted from top down	Granted in all directions
Limited by statute	Unlimited
Given quickly	Earned slowly
Removed slowly by due process	Lost quickly if misused
Written	Unwritten
Formal	Informal
Not value related	Value related
Involuntary	Voluntary
Restricted (closed)	Unrestricted (open)
Extrinsic	Intrinsic

We are looking at authority as the basic concept of a manager; people do what those in positions of authority tell them to do because they are in higher positions than those who aren't in authority. This could be the vice president, marketing manager, line supervisor, sergeant, and so on. Generally it takes a while to get to a position of authority. Authority is given from the top down in an organization and given through promotion or a legal, statutory, contracted process. You do not need leadership traits to have authority, but I'll bet you already knew that from experience!

Power is a totally different concept. It is possible for a person at the bottom of the organization to have more power than the supervisor or manager in charge. It can exist for a number of reasons, for example, because the rest of the employees trust them more, they are more competent, or other employees have more respect for them. It is possible for a middle manager to have more power than someone in upper management for the same reasons.

Blaine Lee describes legitimate power in the same way; he says people follow wholeheartedly and willingly. Lee describes these factors with different names, but the concepts we are discussing are the same. Power is given by the followers in the form of trust, respect, and belief that the leader has their best interests in mind. This bond of followers to leaders is easily broken if the leader breaks that trust or the shared values with the group. Power is maintained with the group while operating according to shared values and goals. This is an example of the group and the leaders working together for a common purpose, vision, or mission. It can correlate to the same principle we discussed in the shared responsibility of learning and teaching. This power can be lost in an instant and may never be regained.

In reviewing "Zen and the Art of Management," we discussed the scenario that employees are rewarded with implied recognition in the form of trust that they can handle more complex and important tasks, thereby creating trust toward the leader. As the leader gives away more trust and power, the follower gives more in return. Power would seem to be a reciprocal investment of trust and confidence in the follower and therefore the definition of empowerment. We talked about the use of ambiguity and the thought of manipulating the followers. What do you suppose will happen to power if a group thinks that it is being manipulated or used by the leader in any fashion?

How important is trust to power? Here's a thought: "Trust is the emotional glue that binds followers and leaders together. The accumulation of trust is a measure of the legitimacy of leadership. It cannot be mandated or purchased, it must be earned. Trust is the basic ingredient of all organizations... It is as mysterious and elusive a concept as leadership."[41]

Power is the ability to get people to do things because they trust you and they want to follow you. Savage entered the 918th with authority. He used authority until the group members saw shared values and a commitment to a mission and began to trust their leader. Major Cobb told Savage the group "went to bat for him with the inspector general." He said that they finally realized they had a chance to complete the mission and return safely when he was leading. Savage's authority to manage the 918th was there in the beginning and throughout his tenure as base commander. By

---

[41] Bennis, Warren, and Nanus, Burt, *Leaders: The Strategies for Taking Charge* (New York: Harper and Row, 1985), 153.

contrast, his *power* to lead the group was only present after the group trusted and respected him as the leader.

Trust and respect, the bond between leaders and followers, is not a simple thing to describe. It involves so many things that it will take us the rest of the book to understand how that bond is formed. Just simply giving out more meaningful tasks is not going to do it. Being a hard-tailed wing commander is not going to do it either. What is required is a balance of leadership values, traits, and management skills that is difficult to find.

Twelve O'Clock High is a theatrical example and a study piece for leadership. "Leadership Aboard the Raider Atlantis"[42] was an article used to give us a look at the relationship of trust, loyalty, and respect with discipline. The tale of the German ship *Raider Atlantis* gives us a real example to discuss power, authority, and sources of power.

Raider Atlantis was a German ship disguised to look like a merchant vessel during WWII. Its crew of 350 set sail in March of 1940, intent on attacking allied vessels, and was at sea for 655 days. Admiral Bernhard Rogge commanded the ship and was quite successful in his mission.

Rogge said that his crew members "had to be trained, educated, persuaded, and won over so that they would do the tasks voluntarily. Only if a man freely accepted the requirements of the service, could the aim be achieved; that he would follow his leaders voluntarily, readily and loyally." Rogge clearly recognized the need to operate on a power basis, not just with authority.

Rogge also said, "Nothing has a stronger influence on the crew than the behavior of the officers and the example they set." He explained that he "selected officers with backbone, professional skill, personality, unselfishness, tact and discretion ... and [they had to] be willing to accept the education which [would] develop the qualities of chivalry, humility, amiability, helpfulness, respect, consideration towards others, reverence and kindness."

---

[42] Rogge, Bernhard, "Leadership Aboard the Raider Atlantis," from *Proceedings* (US Naval Institute, 1963).

He thought the same standards for officers needed to be applied equally to the crew; a similar thought emerges in the pages of "Zen and the Art of Management." Rogge said he adopted this motto: *You cannot be everybody's friend but you can be a good comrade to all.* He told his officers that they were trustees of the men in their charge and that they were officers who were duty bound to their honor. He asked them to constantly examine themselves and correct for errors, to be as honest with themselves as possible.

These might not be very popular ideas in business today, and these ideas may not be stressed by management. But that could be a reason we are lacking good managers and honest, trustworthy leadership. Rogge was following an old Prussian general's philosophy on leadership; once again, there is nothing really new about leadership.

Rogge said that "a man commanding authority who desires to become a true leader cannot take the task of gaining his subordinates' confidence seriously enough. Confidence begets courage; confidence gives strength; confidence produces respect. Nothing can replace it; it is the means toward achieving the greatest things."

Rogge showed the crew he cared by being sure the ship was outfitted with comfortable quarters, sufficient washrooms, shower facilities, berths, ample locker space, reading rooms, a library, a large mess hall, recreation areas, a barber shop, a shoe shop, a tailor shop, laundry facilities, and a large galley and bakery; he even installed an ice cream machine, soda fountain, and refrigerators for beer. He constantly strived to provide training and educational lectures, games, hobbies, and movies. He maintained a focus on the individuals' needs so he could show he cared about each person. When the crews' refrigerator failed and they got warm beer, so did all the officers; everyone was treated as equals but not the same.

Rogge talks about one sailor who was older, but not of any rank or special position. He said this man was respected by the crew. He said he had the crews' "confidence." He said this man was invaluable at times of discontent in that he had the ability (power) to talk with men as an equal, not as a superior, and gain their confidence to maintain order. He was a perfect example of power without authority.

There is lots of material available to look at from the *Raider Atlantis*. The short article we used provides a good background for discussion of the concepts. We will come back to it for some further discussion later.

Zen and the Art of Motorcycle Maintenance[43]

Robert Pirsig's book *Zen and the Art of Motorcycle Maintenance* is very deep and is used in many college courses on philosophy. At first, I found it difficult to read and understand. Then, I met other people who had read it a number of times and just loved it. So, I read it again and again, and now I love it too. I had a lot of people in my class threaten me for making them read it, and a few who just got frustrated and refused to read it. It was the fourth book assigned as required reading for the course.

I can tell you that the book is a challenge to read, but it will make you a better person for reading it. I believe it will open your mind to areas you did not think about and challenge you to explore things you did not know existed. The experience is different when you want to read it as opposed to when you have to read it. Mind-set is everything in learning. It is amazing what you can learn about leadership from a work like *Zen*. Once again, it is not how to *be* a leader, but how to learn to *think* like a leader.

The book is a journey through philosophy and thought. It is disguised as a motorcycle trip across country with the author, his son, and another couple. It is a discussion of quality, art, science, underlying values, meanings, and more. I would like to highlight just a few of the thoughts and concepts I think are valuable leadership traits and insights.

Have you ever bought a new car and just gotten so excited about the beauty and workmanship? After you drive it away you carefully begin to dive into the workings of the car and look at it closely. You begin to use the features and electronics, and feel the ride, handling, performance, and

---

[43] Pirsig, Robert M., *Zen and the Art of Motorcycle Maintenance* (New York: Bantam Books, 1975).

comfort. You begin to find little things you don't like too. *Why did they put that switch there?*, you wonder. You find something that does not work the way you expected it to and flaws in the paint. You go back to the dealership and the dreaded service department. As time goes on, you find other stuff that annoys you—maybe to the point that the car loses the original beauty it had in your mind and you wish you could return it and start over.

Pirsig talks about the danger of placing the knife—the knife of knowledge and science. He describes the experience of Mark Twain and his fascination with the river and the riverboat, and his dream of being a riverboat captain. It is a magical dream to master the beauty of the river. But as he begins to learn all the intricacies of the river, navigation, systems, and so on, it begins to lose its beauty.

He describes the problem with dissecting things. That is what some people do: they want to know what is inside and what makes it work, so they dissect it into smaller parts and pieces to see what the underlying forms are; however, in that process, they lose some of the beauty. Some people never dissect things; they just look at the beauty of the whole and accept it; they need no further information. John and Sylvia (the other couple riding with Pirsig) are the folks who see the world with that perspective while Pirsig tries to dissect the meanings, find the underlying forms, and discover quality.

Knowing that there are different ways of looking at the situation and understanding the difference in the art and science perspectives is an important trait in a leader. Knowing that "placing the knife" will result in a change is important. When you enter into a new organization, it may appear to be beautiful and perfect; but as you get to know the systems, the people, and the policies, that may all change, and the beauty may be lost. It is important to know that when you start "placing the knife," the beauty will be lost for some others in the organization, and it will create a different view of you as the leader.

Pirsig talks about the different views you get on a motorcycle and in a car. He says that essentially you are in a compartment while riding in a car; by contrast, on a motorcycle, you are in the scene, in touch with everything. Clearly this analogy is meant to be transferred to our lives; we sometimes keep ourselves out of touch with everything, tucked away in the safety of our cars, rather than getting out into the environment. This notion has a direct bearing on leadership. Leaders cannot lead from compartments; they must be involved and get the feeling for the whole picture, not just what you see through the windshield. It develops understanding, that *aha* we are looking for.

Pirsig discusses gumption traps; things that we tend to get trapped in that cause us to lose our focus and desire. He describes gumption traps as anything that causes someone to lose sight of quality or enthusiasm for what he or she is doing. As you can imagine, this is a very wide open field of study. Pirsig refers to it as Gumptionology 101.

Pirsig explains how "stuckness" affects us; we get stuck on things and can't seem to get past them. The analogy he uses to explain is a screw that is stuck in the side case of the motorcycle engine; you need to consider all the options to avoid damaging the case while removing the screw. He then applies this concept to interpersonal relationships and business, suggesting that people take a break while trying to figure things out in a difficult relationship so that they don't create more damage to the relationship, themselves, or, if applicable, the organization.

According to Pirsig, we often put a cheap veneer on things to hide what is underneath. I found this an especially helpful way to think about the quick fixes for management and leadership and see them for what they are: cheap veneer to cover something much more complex. Most people do not want to take the time to look into the real problems, only what they need to get done quickly. Taking time to think and get to the real issues will help us to learn to lead.

The book is literally filled with such analogies of life. You can open up to just about any page and start there; you will see something that applies to your life and to being a leader. This book does not tell you how to get past these issues. I have said that you should avoid any book that tells you how to be a leader or how to solve your problems. Everything is so complex, and all situations so different that you need to learn how to think—not how to orchestrate quick fixes. This book will cause you to think your own way out of situations, and it can help you recognize how to avoid frustration and act proactively instead of reactively.

I felt the book told me to stop and smell the roses. I think sometimes we get too wound up in how and why things work. We need to stop and appreciate the beauty of the whole. Maybe that refers to how well the team is working together, what great attributes the team members have, how well the organization is performing, or just how wonderful your family and friends are. The book taught me there is so much to know and appreciate that we must get outside ourselves to learn and see both the art and the science in our search for quality.

I had a friend read the section about stuckness while looking over my shoulder as I was writing this section. She had to read it a couple of times to understand it, and now she thinks I am nuts too! I cannot explain the book, but I am amazed every time I pick it up and read it. The entire book is a search for quality, and it is worth your time to give it a try someday.

Review and Evaluation

For this chapter, I would love for you to watch *Twelve O'Clock High* and relate the movie to the concepts we are exploring here. Consider the concepts of Theory X and Theory Y, accountability and responsibility, as well as all the other questions raised in the discussion.

I would like you to review situations in which you see loyalty conflicts and incongruent value communications in your day-to-day activities. Look for situations where you can use ambiguity and the concepts of implied recognition to empower people.

Always make this about you. Do not confess the sins of others but instead take a look into how you are reacting, what messages you are sending, and what you are loyal to. When you see an example in someone else, try to compare yourself to that situation and choose what you would do in that place.

A word of caution here: do not go to work tomorrow or get the kids out of bed thinking you are General Frank Savage. You do not want to be the kind of person who returns from a one-day seminar with a tough-guy attitude. Keep an eye on the big picture and all the concepts we are exploring, especially humility.

If you want to empower people, explain to them what you are doing; for example, "Chris, you did a really great job on that project, so I am going to trust you with another very important assignment." Explain to Chris the parameters and the flexibility of the assignment. Explain what you think, being aware that ambiguity can be used here. Tell Chris to be creative and keep you informed of the direction and progress. Meet with Chris, make her the center of attention, and ignore the phone and other distractions. Let her know you really care and trust her.

Notes

Chapter Three

Choosing Who I Want to Be

One thing you cannot do is be someone you are not. Leaders do not need to be tough guys. Leaders are kind and compassionate, but they still hold people accountable. If you are trying to be someone you are not, others will see through the façade, and you will lose any trust you are building. So, we are going to start here by exploring who we are and how we demonstrate this to others.

The Self-Fulfilling Prophecy

In Greek mythology Pygmalion was a sculptor who set out to make a statue of the perfect woman. He fell in love with the statue, and the Goddess Venus granted his wish to turn the statue into a real woman, Galatea.

The concept of the Pygmalion Effect (or the Rosenthal Effect) came from a study by psychologist Robert Rosenthal and educator Lenore Jacobson (1968/1992)[44] on the effects of one person's expectations on the performance of another. The idea is that the greater the expectation of success by the teacher, manager, leader, or parent, for example, the better the student, employee, or child will perform. The opposite is also true; if a person has low expectations, this will affect the other person, resulting in a worse performance. The concept is demonstrated in the movie *My Fair Lady* (from the play *Pygmalion* by Shaw) in which a poor woman from

---

[44] Rosenthal, Robert, and Jacobson, Lenore, *Pygmalion in the Classroom*, (New York: Irvington, 1992).

the streets, Eliza Doolittle, is transformed into a lady of society by Henry Higgins, a professor of elocution.

We have discussed the ways that we communicate our values and incongruent value communications. This theory demands consideration because so much is communicated through body language and not necessarily with the words we say. Some communication experts claim that up to 93 percent of communication is body language and paralinguistic clues; others place the percentage at about 70 percent or higher, but either way the majority of our communication comes through nonverbal means.

Rosenthal proposed that people somehow sense our expectations by our actions, and that has an affect on how they perform. In Rosenthal's experiments, teachers were convinced the students could meet high expectations; they were told that one set of students had very high IQs (whether they did or not). In another group, the teachers were told the students were poor learners. In the end, the group with high expectations outperformed the group with low expectations.

The idea of a self-fulfilling prophecy seems valid. If we tell everyone that the banks are in danger of failing, we can create a run on the banks, and they may fail as a result. Years ago in Orange County, California, the county treasurer made some risky investments that went badly. Cities began to pull out of county investments. The media ran stories of huge losses, which caused even more cities to pull their investments. As a result, the county went into bankruptcy. Had no one panicked, the investments would have come back, and the county and cities would have eventually made more money than they had invested. If you tell someone they are not expected to do well in a race, they may not try as hard. If you tell someone they can fight off their cancer, it may cause them to rally and beat the illness. It seems that Rosenthal's theory does have a place in the mind-set of the developer-leader. Even though we can sense others' expectations, we still have a choice about how to react to them. It may even be that lack of expectation that motivates someone to prove they can do a good job on a task or project.

Consider another key point about leadership: *Leaders need to inspire, motivate, trust, and empower followers and clearly communicate those values.* That means we must set high expectations and be confident that our followers can achieve those goals. We must be compassionate, understanding, and patient while still expecting excellence.

The leader's job is to demonstrate confidence in those he or she leads, which can inspire the followers to have confidence. The way we give out assignments, delegate tasks, and present ideas, projects, or goals will affect how our followers process the tasks. We need to take the time to explain the assignments, expectations, and timelines, and give feedback, encouragement, and assistance when it is needed. Doing the job yourself might be easier but would be much less productive in the long term. Leaders are always focused on the long term and on the development of their followers. Doing it this way is much more work, but I never said this was going to be easy.

How can you be sure that you communicate properly and avoid the pitfalls of the Pygmalion Effect and incongruent value communications? For this I go back to *Zen and the Art of Motorcycle Maintenance*, in which Pirsig is in search of quality. The whole book is a search for quality and a comparison of art and science. A simple explanation of how art and science are combined into quality involves caring—not a superficial caring or the cheap veneer of pretending we have quality, but a deep sincere caring, compassion for the task and the people, and a true belief in the abilities of the individual or group.

Pirsig talks about the motorcycle mechanic who doesn't really care and does only what he must to fix the problem. He contrasts this with the mechanic who cares about his work and spends the appropriate amount of time to fix the motorcycle (you realize he is not talking about just a motorcycle). This involves looking at the whole rather than just the parts. Someone who has a genuine love of his or her work and of the motorcycle is likely to do more quality work. That person will be someone you can trust. Can you see a parallel with caring for your followers? Can showing that you sincerely care about them create loyalty, trust, empowerment, power, inspiration, excitement, and enthusiasm? *Leaders genuinely love their followers.*

Yes, I am going to use the L word. When the people who work for you tell you that they love you, you just might be a leader. I am not talking about love in the sense of romance, but in the sense of deep caring about the individuals who put their trust in you to lead. And I am not talking about being easy on them to make them love you. Kouzes and Posner said about respect and liking, "If we absolutely can't have both liking and respect, then we'll choose liking over respect."[45] I would not agree with them on this issue. Machiavelli claims that "one ought to be both feared and loved."[46] He adds that "friendship which is gained by purchase and not through grandeur and nobility of spirit is bought but not secured." It appears to me he is talking about being liked versus being respected. I think we are trying to get to the point of being loved and respected, and we will need to visit Machiavelli later on.

Heroes and Leaders

Jay Mathews wrote, *Escalante: The Best Teacher in America*,[47] about Jaime Escalante, who started off teaching math at Garfield High School in Los Angeles. Escalante began working at Garfield High in 1974, expecting to teach computers; instead he was assigned to basic math. Around 1980 he chose to begin teaching his students an Advanced Placement calculus program. The first class, which he taught during the 1981–82 school year, brought him into the limelight with accusations of cheating by the Educational Testing Service, which administered the test. Subsequently, Hollywood immortalized him in the movie *Stand and Deliver*,[48] with his character played by Oscar-nominee Edward James Olmos. Escalante was the consummate developer, a perfect model of leadership and the "post-heroic" developer concept described by David Bradford and Allan Cohen

---

[45] Kouzes, James M., and Posner, Barry Z., *A Leader's Legacy* (San Francisco: Jossey-Bass A. Wiley, 2006), 58.

[46] Machiavelli, *The Prince*.

[47] Mathews, Jay. *Escalante: The Best Teacher in America* (New York: Henry Holt & Co., 1988)

[48] *Stand and Deliver*, Warner Bros Pictures, 1988.

in *Managing for Excellence*.[49] *Managing for Excellence*, the fifth book we used in the leadership program, is an exploration of how we develop others.

Escalante spent many years at Garfield High, but the effort to operate in the post-heroic/developer mode took its toll on him. He grew weary of the constant battles, fighting those who failed to understand his method of teaching, and eventually moved to Sacramento, California. He taught there for his remaining years. Leaders, such as Escalante, tend to be thinkers ahead of their time, operating in a leadership mode that is not widely understood. Their ideas and methods may be rejected or challenged as Escalante's were.

Some of our program instructors got to meet Escalante during a facilitator meeting in Sacramento. During our meeting Escalante explained that he was not teaching math, he was teaching how to think and how to learn, by using math as his vehicle. Kids who were taught by Escalante were usually very successful in life. His own children became civil and electrical engineers. He had many students pass the AP Calculus test. What intrigued Jay Mathews to research and write about him was not the accusations of cheating; it was the fact that Escalante was doing so much with so little in the way of resources that Mathews had to find out how it was working.

Bradford and Cohen describe several management styles in *Managing for Excellence*. One is the manager as a technician. That is the typical style, in which the manager is very specialized in an area and usually very good at the task; this manager could be excellent at running various machines or completing computer programming tasks, closing sales, or any number of things. It is quite typical that managers get hired or promoted because they have technical expertise in a particular area.

There is a lot to be said about the manager-as-technician style. Credibility and competence are qualities we want to see in our leaders. Kouzes and Posner said they found that credibility was the number-one thing people

---

[49] Bradford, David L., and Cohen, Allan R., *Managing for Excellence*, (New York: John Wiley and Sons, 1984).

looked for in leaders.[50] I do not support the idea that if you are a good manager then you can manage anything. I compare that to being a good teacher who does not read or understand music theory. How is that teacher going to teach or lead music with any real credibility?

What we do not want are technicians who keep knowledge to themselves. We do not want them having to come to the rescue of the workers who should be doing the tasks. This is why Bradford and Cohen refer to it as a *heroic* style of leadership. It is very common for the workers to rely on the technician and therefore stifle the growth, creativity, and development of the followers. Technicians can find it easier to do tasks themselves rather than develop their followers to excel at those same tasks. It can become necessary for the technician to take over in an emergency situation.

The conductor is another management style described by Bradford and Cohen. In the conductor style, the manager is at the center of a group, and everything must go through him or her. The conductor is the only person who has the big picture and understands all the parts of the process. This method also stifles growth, creativity, and development, and probably slows down production too. This may work well in an emergency situation where information sharing is not important or information is purposely kept confidential. It is not a style that promotes productivity, independent thinking, or development of followers.

In his classroom Escalante involved everyone in the learning process. He was inspiring. He always told them, "You can do it." He told his students that all they needed was *ganas* (desire). Escalante's methods, as well as Bradford and Cohen's post-heroic model, are in sync with McGregor's Theory Y. In all cases, these leaders trust their people to accomplish the tasks. In all cases they strive for the development of followers to excel beyond the leaders' own accomplishments and progress beyond their own expectations (Pygmalion at work here!).

---

[50] Kouzes, James, and Posner, Barry, "Eye of the Follower," *Administrative Radiology*, April 1986, 55–64.

Bradford and Cohen's post-heroic leadership style places the responsibility on the followers for learning, production, improvement, process, management, and overall success of the project. It seems to tie into the issues we looked at in "Zen and the Art of Management," power and empowerment, BLTs, and so forth. People need to be involved in the process, have some control over the process, know that their ideas are important, and be in control of themselves. If I am not in control of anything, then I just show up and do my eight hours and go home, all the while looking forward to doing something I have control over. Bradford and Cohen talk about how important it is to move subordinates beyond the minimum levels and above the mundane. They say, "There must be a purpose—a reason that they should give that extra effort."[51]

Bradford and Cohen also warn about highly motivated people and the risk of conflicts. People working together will inevitably have differing opinions. This will require a leader who is patient, compassionate, and understanding to help resolve differences by identifying what is at the core of a problem (underlying issues from the Zen book). It is important to have members of a group learn how to identify and resolve issues themselves if they are going to move through the stages of team development. Additionally, "people may be willing to put up with frustration, incompetence and bureaucratic delays from management if they are not personally invested or [if they] merely perform at minimum levels."[52] However, when they become committed to quality, they are going to expect everyone in the loop to also be committed, and they will become less tolerant of slackers or incompetent leadership.

In Escalante's classroom everyone participated and was held accountable for participation by the group. Escalante built that teamwork in his classroom. This is not something that happens without hard work; it involves trust and respect for the leader, who must demonstrate and inspire the group to a common purpose. Bradford and Cohen refer to this as an overarching goal, but others would call it vision. For example, in Escalante's classroom the goal was to not end up working as *taco vendors*

---

[51] Bradford and Cohen, *Managing for Excellence*, 85.
[52] Ibid., 71–2.

for the rest of their lives, but instead to pass AP Calculus on their way to engineering or other science degrees and successful lives and careers.

A leader always operates in a developer mind-set. Leaders are always looking for opportunities to develop followers. It helps to have an unselfish mind-set also, so you are not looking for opportunities to make yourself look good. Realize that if you are doing the right thing by developing your followers, someone will notice.

Escalante showed his students that math was a necessity for school, work, and a future in their world. He showed them that they could do it, though it would not be easy, and he helped instill the desire in them. He showed them the future would be unlimited for them if they believed in themselves.

Consider this scene: When one of Escalante's students wants to drop out of school and become an auto mechanic, Escalante takes the student for a drive. He forces him to choose a turn, but that choice leads to a dead-end street. Escalante tells him that he only sees the turn and not the road ahead.

Escalante was good at not taking the short-term approach but instead looking into the long-term and communicating that to his kids. He was good at providing the overarching goal, or a vision of the future, making it real and significant in the lives of his followers.

Savage does the same thing with Lieutenant Bishop in *Twelve O'Clock High*. He lays out the long-term vision of the bomber group and explains what significance Bishop and he play in that goal; it is part of team building. Both Savage and Escalante keep the team focused on the goal, operating in the circle of influence, focused on quality, avoiding gumption traps, and performing to the top of their abilities.

Escalante loved his kids; he put his heart and soul into helping to make them successful. I encourage you to watch the movie or read Jay Mathew's book. Escalante was an incredible leader who incurred the wrath and jealousy of other teachers, administrators, gangs, and dangerous students, and even suffered health issues as a result of his all-giving, unselfish leadership style. You will see the same traits and caring in General Savage and just about every other great leadership example you look at. Are you ready for this type of commitment?

What Teams Share

Our goal as leaders is to build shared responsibility teams. On the *Raider Atlantis*, Admiral Rogge was fortunate to have been able to pick his crew. He defined areas that he thought were important, and picked his crew as well as officers that would match his values and be a good fit for the mission. I can tell you that such a scenario is probably not going to happen much at work. You may be saddled with someone who is not going to go along with the program no matter how hard you try.

In those instances you may need to cut that person loose and allow them to accept the consequences of their actions. It is important that we do not allow someone to stifle the rest of the team. Just be careful you are not cutting loose a Jonathan or someone who has a lot to offer just because you don't like the haircut, so to speak. In *Stand and Deliver*, Hollywood took creative license with parts of the story to add drama and entertainment, but most of Jaime Escalante's students were high achievers. Always remember Pygmalion and don't place people in prejudicial boxes unless you are prepared to face Sundance and go through a significant emotional event, such as a lawsuit. A manager may kick aside a diamond thinking it is a rock, but leaders always look closer and recognize diamonds when they see them.

If you have a problem with someone on your team, you need to address it. If, as a leader, you avoid people, you cannot have an impact on their development. It is necessary to confront troublesome situations and try to resolve them. Everyone on a given team must feel comfortable with the other members, and that includes the leader. How can you love these people if you can't stand them? You have control over your actions. You set the goals and expectations, and allow them to perform. In all cases you need to provide feedback to the group and to the individuals. Bradford and Cohen say this about feedback:

Many attempts at giving feedback, particularly around another's interpersonal style, do not work because the giver of the feedback does not stick with this area of expertise (how the behavior affects them) but moves into the other's area of expertise (the intention of the behavior).[53]

That means that we should not say, "You did [whatever the specific error was]." Instead we should approach it by explaining how we felt or perceived the incident. This allows the person to not feel as challenged by the leader and allows for some explanation of the intent. It provides an opportunity for the follower to develop and for the leader to demonstrate caring. It also helps to ensure that the feedback is genuinely designed to be helpful rather than become an opportunity to punish and criticize. Feedback is a necessary component in all team development.

To build this shared-responsibility team, all members must share the overarching goal or vision. Members must understand they are responsible for the success and control of the mission. The greater the challenge and responsibility, the more effort the team will put into a quality solution. The key here is transferring the responsibility for success or failure to the team. The leader's job is to help the team to succeed by helping members grow or develop in the process and making sure the recognition for excellence goes to the team.

One element of a shared-responsibility team is that everyone is aware of everyone else's responsibilities. That is something that keeps us alive in police work, knowing and trusting that we all carry out our responsibilities. On a silent alarm call, for example, I know that my back-up officer will respond to the opposite corner of the building, and we will coordinate to cover all the exits. I know that if the back-up officer fails to do this properly, we will have a feedback session. Our lives and the safety of many people depend on us doing it right.

I once took a group of motorcycle officers to film some public service announcements with the US Air Force Thunderbirds precision flying

---

[53] Ibid., 155.

team. The team had just finished a practice flight and met with us briefly before the debriefing. We offered to wait until they were finished with the debriefing, but they told us that the process could take awhile. Because of their shared-responsibility team, when they debriefed, they were not shy about discussing poor performance. They talked to each other about who was not up to the standard of excellence and what they needed to do to improve. That is what shared-responsibility teams do. A team knows what each member is responsible for, and they hold each other accountable, they do not place blame. They work together to solve problems and to excel as a team.

Bradford and Cohen define stages of group development that are similar to other works on stages of group identification and development. They are membership, subgrouping, confrontation, differentiation, and shared responsibility. They say that at the group's initial get-together members tend to be very shy until they begin to identify people that want to associate with in subgroups. The subgroups tend to fight for control and influence until some technical expertise emerges and they begin to clarify goals. Once that happens the group may be headed for shared responsibility. (This is an ultra-simplified description of the process that we will explore in chapter 6 with group dynamics.)

In the leadership program, I would always take the opportunity at the end of session three to ask the participants where they thought we were with respect to group development. Most thought that we were at the shared-responsibility stage. Occasionally, some members would say they did not believe we had progressed to that stage and challenge other members about how much effort they had put into presentations, homework, class projects, and the like.

From the facilitator's perspective I can say that it was very rare that we were anywhere close to shared responsibility in session three. Most groups were still in a subgrouping stage. Some classes never progressed past the subgroups; others progressed to various stages, and some even made it to shared responsibility. Every class was the same, yet different. The material did not really change—only the people and their desire.

Bradford and Cohen are very real and recognize that the reactions will vary from "discomfort in stage one, suspicion in stage two, hostility in stage three, to foot-dragging in stage four—but the reaction will seldom be unalloyed enthusiasm. However, a manager should not be discouraged by such reactions, but take them as an indication of how important it is to move the group beyond where they are at the present."[54] Not everyone in Escalante's classes passed the AP Calculus test. Cunningham would always remind me to not be disappointed if the group did not make it to shared responsibility but to enjoy how much improvement they demonstrated in the process. Remember that we are striving for excellence, not necessarily perfection.

The Inner Game

So, if you are like me, you are probably wondering, "Just how the heck am I supposed to remember all this stuff and incorporate it into everyday work to be that great leader I want to be?" The simple answer is, *You can't!* It is not possible to do this from memory. Remember it is not simply a set of skills anyone can be taught. It is a set of values and traits that you learn, live, and act upon in everyday life.

One day I was at the driving range hitting some golf balls, pretending to be Tiger Woods but looking more like Bill Murray, when I overheard the golf pro a couple of mats down giving some instruction to someone. It caught my attention because I heard him say, "You just have to relax and let 'Self 2' take over." Suddenly I realized he was teaching from Tim Gallwey's book, *The Inner Game of Golf.*

I thought, "This is so great—someone who actually believes in Gallwey's *Inner Game* stuff." I am also a believer in the *Inner Game* stuff. We used Gallwey's book, *The Inner Game of Tennis,*[55] as the sixth book in the leadership program. Both books are very similar except for the sizes of the balls and playing fields. We began by working on developing ourselves through identification of values. *The Inner Game of Tennis* continues exploring how we develop ourselves.

---

54 Ibid., 203.
55 Gallway, W. Timothy, *The Inner Game of Tennis,* (New York: Random House, 1974).

Gallwey talks about the judgmental self, "Self 1." He says we all have our conscious Self 1, who always wants to be in control, criticizing, evaluating, and controlling our moves. However, inside is our subconscious, "Self 2." Self 2 sees everything that Self 1 does but without the controlling and constant critical evaluation of Self 1.

Have you ever gotten "in the zone"? It is that place where you are just doing something—and doing it well—but not thinking about it. You have put up the filters, tuned everything out, and are just cruising. It could be when you are out on a run, just cruising along without thinking, only to be amazed, when you reach the end, that it seemed so effortless. Or it could be when you are racing, playing a game, reading a book, or doing any number of things where you just lose track of what else is going on. Gallwey says that is Self 2 at work.

Now back to the golf course. I put my head down and concentrate on the dimples on the golf ball. I am not really trying to make a great swing; but I get great contact, and my buddies tell me, "That was a great swing." The ball goes way down the fairway; I just outdrove everyone with a three-wood. How? I've got no clue, but I really want to do it again! So I set up the next time and start thinking about how I made that swing: *What did I do? How can I repeat it?* Can you guess what happens? Yep, that ball goes off to the right of the women's tee, and the game takes an embarrassing turn from there. Gallwey would say I let Self 1 come back and take over.

I'm recounting this story to illustrate to you that trying to memorize leadership traits and values is not going to work. These things must be values that you hold dear and that you don't need to think about. They have to become a part of your life, your very being, or you will not get your ball off the tee. Gallwey talks about how you need to look for the seams on the tennis ball and hit the seams with the racket. You need to visualize it and let Self 2 make the approach on the ball and make the swing for you. In the same way, you need to internalize these values of leadership so that they naturally form the basis for the way you respond to situations—without you having to think about it.

Gallwey asks, "How can I just let the forehand happen if I have never learned how to hit one in the first place? Don't I need someone to tell me how to do it? If I've never played tennis before, can I just go out on the court and let it happen? The answer is: if your body knows how to hit a forehand, then just let it happen; if it doesn't, then just let it learn."[56] He is telling us that Self 2 knows a lot of stuff from watching and recording events, whether playing tennis or golf, or managing and leading. Gallwey is also saying that what we don't know, we need to allow ourselves to learn. This goes back to our learning theory and having the humility to recognize what you don't know.

Gallwey's books are short, and easy to read and understand. They will prove to be a resource that will help you in many situations. I cannot guarantee your games will improve, but you will know which game you are playing. Gallwey ends his book with a list of games we play in our heads, such as

- Fun-o, a game (rarely played in its pure form!) that is played neither for winning nor to become good at it, but merely for the fun alone, and
- Compete-o, a game played to prove I am better than you; this game is played only against the other players, with no set standard of excellence.[57]

You've probably guessed there is more to Gallwey's books than helping you play tennis or golf!

Honesty

The thought of playing games with people also brings up the issue of how we play the game. Our ethical behavior is an important issue in leadership. Kouzes and Posner say that followers want leaders who are honest, competent, forward looking, inspiring, and credible.[58] Leadership consultant John Zenger said that a leader needs to be an example for his or

---

[56] Gallwey, W. Timothy, *The Inner Game of Tennis* (New York: Random House, 1974), 53.
[57] Ibid., 108–10.
[58] Kouzes and Posner, "Eye of the Follower," 55–64.

her followers and that the most dramatic model of this was a leader who told his people "they could do anything that they saw him doing."[59]

We can discuss honesty, but we all pretty much know what that means. When your wife asks, "Does this dress make me look fat?" the correct answer is ... what? Certainly honesty is the best policy, but maybe not in that case! Sissela Bok wrote a book called *Lying: Moral Choices in Public and Private Life*.[60] It is an interesting piece of work. Most people will lie to save themselves and in our society that seems to be acceptable—would you agree?

I can't begin to tell you the amount of people who will lie to get out of a ticket. Most cops are so impressed with people who admit a mistake that those folks get away without a citation. If I am greeted with, "Why did you stop me?," there is a good chance the situation is not going to end well for the violator. (In the business, we just say, "Press hard, three copies.") Like most people, I hate to be lied to. If you want to lose credibility, just lie to your followers. All those months and years of building trust can be lost in a heartbeat. You can pretty much apply that theory to every relationship you have; lie to your wife, girlfriend, boyfriend, husband, child, or whomever, and the trust is in big trouble.

I think we want to live ethical lives. Who is the most ethical person you know? Is it you? I think most of us would say, "Yes, it is me," but is it really? We only know our true values when those values are tested. Do you speak up in the staff meeting when you know someone is not presenting the facts correctly? If your child committed a violation of the school policy—or a violation of law—would you defend him or admit the error? Does concealing an illegal act create a bond, a loyalty, a friend? Is the person you look up to as the best leader an honest person? Gee, I don't know. I do know that I am not perfect, only Jesus was. I am just forgiven. I try not to be too judgmental of the sins of others, but like everyone, I certainly take all this into account when choosing to follow someone.

---

59 Zenger, John H., "Leadership: Management's Better Half," *Training* 22(12), 44–53.
60 Bok, Sissela, *Lying: Moral Choices in Public and Private Life* (New York: Knopf, 1999).

Code of Silence

For a case study I chose to use the movie *Serpico*.[61] The film is about the life of Frank Serpico, a New York City police officer who uncovered corruption and testified against other officers. It is an interesting movie (based on the real life story of Officer Serpico and the book by Peter Maas) that allows us to look at the code of silence issues in the police department. Everyone knows that cops stick together and protect each other with a code of silence, right? In the world of cops, there seems to be justification for such a code, as it seems like everyone is against them. The film allows us to take a look at a multitude of issues that boil down to value conflicts.

Cops are not the only group that has a code of silence. Try to get doctors to testify against each other (or attorneys, politicians, car salesmen, firemen, nurses, bankers, brokers, teachers—you name it!). There is a code of silence in all professions and jobs. No one wants to be known as a tattletale or a snitch, so everyone keeps quiet. Even with the public at large, when the nicest kid is gunned down in the ghetto, no one ever sees anything.

Is this right? Is it right to cover up someone's illegal activity? We have laws against that, you know. This is a crime called being an accessory after the fact, which basically makes you a conspirator, and guilty of the same offense. Why would you be willing to accept responsibility for something you know is illegal and make yourself a party to the crime? Why would you not want the person or persons responsible to be held accountable and brought to justice? Is it because you don't want to see Harry get fired for his poor performance and judgment, and you are willing to share the consequences with him? Does that sound like the response of someone on a shared-responsibility team? Is courage somehow tied up in all of this? Is it honorable or courageous to conceal an illegal act and join into a code-of-silence cover up? Do you want the top bunk or the bottom bunk in the jail cell?

One group in a class used the film *Scent of a Woman*[62] for their final project. They were trying to show the concept of courage as depicted by

---

[61] *Serpico*, Paramount Pictures, 1973.
[62] *Scent of a Woman*, Universal Studios, 1992.

the character Frank Slade, a blind Army Ranger lieutenant colonel (played by Al Pacino). The movie takes a look at an incident involving a young man attending an elite prep school with an honor code. He witnesses an incident of vandalism (a prank directed at the headmaster) and is ordered to appear at a hearing to identify the suspects, but he refuses to identify them. The colonel represents him at the hearing and tells everyone the young man is the only one of them with any courage because he has refused to be a snitch. I was shocked at the presentation and asked them if we had wasted eight months of class with them?

There is a difference between a tattletale and someone who reports illegal or unethical actions. Have you ever thought about it? Can you tell what it is? When I was a sergeant in patrol, every night one particular officer would come up to me and tell me about what the other officers on his squad were doing behind my back. He felt he was reporting improper behavior, but none of it was illegal, in violation of policy, or anything that required attention. This reporting was all done as a way to make this guy look better (he thought) in the eyes of his supervisor. All of the officers on the team were working hard and catching bad guys, just like they were supposed to do. In fact, they were seriously exceeding the performance of the other squads. Even the snitch was a hard worker—he just had another agenda. Would you consider him a tattletale?

In real life Frank Serpico was an outstanding person. Serpico worked in the police department for years and witnessed numerous acts of corruption—criminal acts, unethical conduct—and did report those acts to superiors on occasion. But the whole system was so corrupt, and the code of silence so ingrained, that he got little or no help. While Frank witnessed many such incidents, he did not want to testify against any other officers and be labeled a snitch. He wanted someone else to build a case, with him supplying insider information. That did not work out well for Serpico; he was forced to testify in a closed grand jury hearing that resulted in a few indictments. Of course the rumors of him being a snitch got around the department. Subsequently, he was assigned to a narcotics detail and was shot in the face by a suspect while other officers stood by. Finally, Serpico testified at the hearings of the Knapp Commission,[63] and many officers were arrested and prosecuted.

Serpico's story makes a great movie, and it happens everyday, everywhere. How is it possible that Enron ran such a scam and fleeced the public out of billions of dollars? People in that company knew what was going on. Brokers across the country knew what was gong on. But no one spoke up until an administrative assistant blew the whistle on the company. How many executives and elected officials can we cite here as examples of a code of silence and corruption? A real lack of ethical leadership exists in this country in all aspects of life, public and private. How do we as leaders make an impact in an organization?

Communicating Organizational Ethics

Harvard Business School professor Kenneth Andrews wrote a short article *Ethics in Practice*[64] in which he discusses ethics in the organization. He discusses how society, schools, sports, parents, and so forth are not teaching ethics to the degree we might expect. That is true if we are expecting them to teach ethics in a positive light. What they may be teaching is a lack of moral values and ethics. There appears to be a void that leaves it up to people to learn on their own how things work. Andrews says that students are no longer attracted to moral philosophy, but instead to economics and personal pleasures. Business schools are including ethical behavior in courses just like we include ethical behavior in the police academy, but is it effective? The problems come when employees get into the business environment on the other side of school. In police work many training officers tell recruits to forget all the stuff they learned in the academy. "This is how it works out here," they say. Similar things happen everywhere no matter what the business or job.

Police professional Michael Hyams[65] presented some very interesting statistics in his research concerning police officers. He said that 26

---

[63] The Knapp Commission (named for the chairman, Whitman Knapp) was set up to investigate police corruption in New York City beginning in 1970.
[64] Andrews, Kenneth R, "Ethics in Practice," *Harvard Business Review*, Sep–Oct 1989.
[65] Hyams, Michael, "Communicating the Ethical Standard," *Journal of California Law Enforcement*, 1991.

percent of incumbent officers and 16 percent of recruit officers admitted they would lie to save a friend's job, but not their own; 45 percent of incumbents and 21 percent of recruits said it was okay to accept gratuities; 12 percent of incumbent officers and 3 percent of recruits would lie on a report; 45 percent of incumbents and 23 percent of recruits would exaggerate probable cause; 39 percent of incumbents and 21 percent of recruit officers were okay with street justice (excessive force); 75 percent of incumbents and 47 percent of recruits were more likely to use abusive or disrespectful language. He said incumbent officers were more likely to ignore minor criminal violations and less likely to take action when misconduct was observed and more protective of fellow officers when misconduct was alleged.

If you take out the reference to police officers and apply that to any other line of work, would you find the percentages to be similar? In the business world that might involve price fixing, recalls, product safety, profit margins, bribery of officials, design, sales, shipping, insider trading, or any number of things. Do people enter into organizations more ethically sound than they are after being there for a while?

In most cases the organization will define the ethics. Most people will do what they need to in order to fit in. Most organizations will have policies, procedures, an organizational value statement, a code of ethics, and so on; however, these things need to be reinforced in other ways. Simply having a written statement is not going to communicate the ethical standard. The people that we have trouble with are always looking for a loophole, something that is not specifically prohibited by written policy. It is a lack of adherence to principles, values, and ethics that is the problem.

Most of the articles on the subject agree that the ethical standard needs to start at the top. The CEO of an organization must clearly communicate the organizational values and standards through their actions and enforcement of those standards. The articles agree that training, swift punishment of violations, internal policies, inspection, and supervision awareness are all necessary. How can we get to people's core values? Can we reach people with a boring PowerPoint presentation on ethics?

Ethics are learned experientially. People need to be placed in situations where they can discuss and discover their own and others' values. In class we use a number of ethical dilemmas for this process, as well as exercises that ask the students to think about all the people or stakeholders the hypothetical decisions and events will affect.

Serpico had firsthand knowledge of the criminal acts and felonies being committed in his presence, but he took no action to stop any of it. Serpico was told by a commander that he could take action and testify, but might wind up face down in the East River. Police officers take their lives into their hands every time they step out on the street. Cops are the people who drive 100 miles per hour to get to a gunfight while everyone else is running away. The reason we call them the city's "finest" is that they are so courageous. So, why was Serpico afraid to report other cops who were involved in criminal activity?

I ask the officers in my class what they would do if a fellow officer came to them with a bribe and asked them to be part of a cover-up or asked them to be a party to a crime. They all say they would report it to a superior and take action to be sure the corrupt officers were arrested. Then we talk about why Serpico didn't arrest the first guy who offered him a bribe? Why did Serpico refuse to testify against the officers he knew were involved in criminal activity and police corruption? Was Serpico a coward?

Gee, talk about running around gunpowder with a blowtorch! You'd think I had suggested overthrow of the government! "Serpico, a coward?" the class members would respond. "How dare you make such a charge!" Of course he was not a coward, but it really opens up a discussion. These are the types of ethics questions you need to discuss in an organization.

Were the executives at Enron—who had to know about the cover-ups, bookkeeping, and false reporting—all cowards? Did they have a duty to the company, the employees, the public, and themselves to come forward and report the criminal behavior? How many instances can you think of in which people covered up, concealed, or just kept quiet about acts they knew of that resulted in corruption? Are they all cowards? Can you be a leader if you are a coward? We need to be blunt, open, and challenging on these points to create value-based discussions in our organizations if we intend to communicate ethical standards.

On day one of every class I facilitated, I made it clear that we expected confidentiality in the class, but that did not mean we would conspire to cover up criminal acts. I told them that if I became aware of a criminal act, I would arrest the offender myself. The CEO of a company can make that clear a statement as well, communicating clearly and concisely, so that there is no doubt about what the values and ethics of the company are. There are people in organizations who will try to take advantage of any loophole or who can be led the wrong way by someone if leaders do not clearly communicate a lack of tolerance for unethical behavior. It is the place of every leader to maintain ethical behavior and demand it from followers. A PowerPoint presentation and a handout are not going to be sufficient to influence people's value systems. It will take an experienced facilitator (or leader) and a group discussion to make it real to participants.

I am going to separate our discussion of ethics into two separate sections. We will pick it up again at the end of chapter 4 after putting more pieces into the matrix. Clearly ethics, values, and principles play a big part in learning leadership. It seems like it should be so simple, but you never really know what you will do until the situation tests you. It is important to have thought about how you should react before the situation arises. In this way you can see the seams on the ball as it comes across the net and Self 2 will hit the perfect backhand before Self 1 has time to analyze the possible advantages of doing the wrong thing. *Leaders set ethical standards by example.*

Review and Evaluation
For chapter 3, please look for situations that demonstrate the Pygmalion Effect, heroic and post-heroic management, and code-of-silence issues. Think about how you would respond. What is your first thought about each situation? Is that your true value? Then think about how you should respond to the situation and how Self 1 and Self 2 are working.

Let's play with a simple exercise that is completely possible and likely to occur in everyone's organizations. Think about how you would handle it and present it to others for their thoughts.

Code of Silence versus Leadership versus Management

Imagine that you are the CFO of your company. You are at home in New York at 2:00 a.m. when the phone rings; it is Tom, the son of a longtime family friend, who you managed to get hired to work in your company's sales department. Tom is a recent graduate with a marketing degree and no experience, but a very promising future. Tom is in Florida at a conference with the sales and marketing teams.

Tom is calling from a hospital, where he and three other members of the sales team are being treated for minor injuries resulting from a car crash. Tom is calling for advice; he is scared and does not know what to do. He tells you that he was in the car with three older representatives; one of them was driving, and Tom thinks he was speeding when they got into the crash. The other party received minor injuries also and was treated and released from the hospital. Tom also thinks he smelled alcohol on the driver when they got into the car and overheard someone say that the driver had been at a party earlier that evening. Tom says he is not sure of any of this, but that the police are there at the hospital investigating the accident.

A senior manager is also in Florida for the conference and has just arrived at the hospital. He is with Tom in the emergency room, so you ask to speak to him. Tom has shared his concerns with this manager, but the manager tells you he can see no evidence of what Tom has shared with the two of you. You have known this manager for a long time, and know he is a trusted, honest person. The manager tells you that, even though he sees no evidence to support Tom's story, he has a gut feeling the sales reps are hiding something. The sales reps are a very close unit and have been known to conceal information when it benefits the group. They have also been known to make life at work impossible for people whom they do not like or who do not fit in with the group. The police have indicated to your manager that they believe the sales rep that was driving may be at fault, but the evidence is inconclusive. They indicate that no action will be taken against either party, and tell you that they are about to leave the hospital.

Tom wants to do the right thing here, but he is not sure what that is. He knows that if he says anything, he will be labeled a snitch, but he does not want to conceal information that might make a difference in the other party's case. You know that the other party will probably take legal action, as your company has deep pockets. You know that Tom will suffer if he says anything and that none of his accusations can be proven. Heck, even Tom is not sure of his accusations.

What would a manager do in this situation? What would a leader do in this situation, and is it different from what a manager would do? Does this commit you to a code-of-silence problem? Is this simply confidentiality? What are the loyalty issues involved? What are the long-term issues involved in this scenario?

The information Tom may have will have no bearing on the case except to provide a reasonable doubt argument for the other party, and put into question the integrity of your driver. Telling Tom to keep the information to himself unless he is sure instantly sets up a code-of-silence issue with you and Tom. And what if Tom says something later? You could both be implicated in a cover-up. If Tom speaks up and the other manager is correct about the group, Tom will never recover from the wrath of the group. A safe thing to do (management?) is to tell Tom to speak up, let the chips fall where they may, and go back to sleep. Leaders are risk takers. Is this a risk you think is proper to take?

Notes

Chapter Four

Taking Control

It's the Principle Worth Fighting for

We have been talking about ethics, values, principles, and morals as they relate to a leader's behavior. It becomes necessary to find some definitions for these "creatures" so we have some common references as to what we are talking about. We need to look at our values and how they affect the choices we make as leaders. These value choices relate to something we call "principle versus preference." To explore this we will need to define some terms.

Is there a difference between tenacious and stubborn? Is there a difference between flexible and wishy-washy? Sure—we all see a difference between those terms. A wishy-washy person really has no clear positions on what they are all about and what they are doing. This person does whatever is most beneficial for himself or herself. We never really know what this person thinks or wants because he or she is afraid to take a stand. Those who are stubborn just refuse to listen to others; these people always know the answer and are going to do it their way.

Someone who is tenacious is a driven individual. Usually we associate tenacity with hard workers who can get things done. Someone who is flexible is a person we can usually work with; he or she is open to suggestions and other points of view. These appear to be good traits and not selfish ones, as stubbornness and wishy-washiness appear to be.

Let us now add a consideration of principle versus preference. If you are flexible on principles, you become wishy-washy, a flip-flopper, a manager who does whatever will make him look the best, someone with only self-interest at heart. If you are tenacious with regard to preferences, you will be seen as stubborn, selfish, closed-minded, and a know-it-all. No one wants to be managed by people like this, nor will they be led by such folks.

We all like to know where we stand and what the rules are, and we want to be sure the rules will be applied equally. We also want to know that our leaders are open to input and options (so this is starting to sound like "Zen and the Art of Management" again). As the leader you can be flexible about preferences but tenacious with respect to principles. Being flexible with preferences makes you approachable; being tenacious about principles makes you predictable. Now all we need to do is figure out what principles, values, and ethics really are.

We look at ethics, values, and principles as different but connected things; for example:

- Principles: the rules that define values, transcend societies and cultures, and are the basis for everything we believe
- Values: our interpretation of the principles
- Ethics: society's interpretation of the principles and shared values (may depend on the society you are in at the time)

Let me try to explain what I mean by this with an example:

- Principle: You shall not kill.
- Value: Killing is wrong, so I will not kill, except in self-defense.
- Ethics: Killing is wrong, but justifiable and acceptable under certain circumstances, including self-defense, defense of others, and capital punishment.

A principle is the basis for the way we define our values. A principle is something that can transcend societies and cultures and is accepted worldwide as good. In our culture, we mostly go back to the Judeo-

Christian values that came from things such as the Ten Commandments, prohibitions against killing, stealing, coveting, lying, committing adultery, and so on. I think these are principles that are accepted in almost all societies as a foundation for what is right. Another principle may be to respect others' rights to life, liberty, and property.

Other people have different interpretations of principles; James Q. Wilson, in his book *The Moral Sense*, describes principles as sympathy, fairness, self-control, and duty, among others; Rushworth Kidder of the *Christian Science Monitor* suggests compassion, fairness, responsibility, honesty, and respect; and from the Josephson Institute comes the "Six Pillars of Character": caring, fairness, responsibility, trustworthiness, respect, and citizenship. The search for what are true principles has been going on since we have recorded thought in any form. It is probably safe to say that no one really has a perfect definition, especially since we all are using our own paradigms to interpret what they are. You should try to make your own list.

Values are how we define the principles and our most deeply held beliefs. If we hold the principle of "Thou shall not kill" to be a deeply held belief or value, then we may not find killing justifiable under any conditions. We have people deeply opposed to the death penalty under any circumstance. Others, however, believe that justice is "an eye for an eye" and killing is acceptable in those instances.

We have people who think that killing is totally justified if you are of a different race or ethnicity. For example, members of the Ku Klux Klan bombed a church in Birmingham, Alabama, in the 1960s and thought nothing of the fact that they killed four young black girls. In the movie *Mississippi Burning,* which addresses the same period in US history, one suspect who was questioned by an FBI agent says that he wouldn't think any more about killing a black person than he would "wringing a chicken's neck."

This same group thinks killing a white person who shares their value system would be wrong and a crime. Killing to them is wrong only if the victim is someone who shares their values. Maybe this is based on the thought that people who do not share their value system are not human beings and therefore they do not feel it is wrong to kill them. Yet they still know it is a criminal act. Do you want to go back to the discussion of the gang members who grow up in the ghetto supposedly not knowing it is wrong to steal? If they don't think stealing is a criminal act, why do they conceal it?

A gang may go out and kill or steal from another group, but these same actions are considered completely unacceptable within the gang. A tribe of cannibals may eat outsiders but not each other. The point is that they all understand the principle of it not being acceptable to kill; they just apply the principle differently because of their values. Can this apply to lying, stealing, bribery, and other issues we face daily in business?

I think that your values are your unreasoned responses—in other words, your first thought when you see a situation. Your initial thought may be your value, but it can be tempered by the ethics of the society. Ethics are the accepted standard that society puts on an interpretation of the principles. An example could be justifiable homicide. American society accepts the killing of a person in self-defense or defense of others; it is also considered acceptable in cases where the state has judged a person guilty of a capital crime.

Your values may not agree with this society's ethic. You may still feel it is wrong to kill under any circumstances, even in self-defense. A gang member may still think it is just fine to kill a member of another gang, but then society may impose its ethical standard on him in the form of the death penalty or imprisonment. Ethics can change. Laws do change. Our society is still debating the ethical-moral dilemma of the death penalty. This debate goes on by majority rule, legislation, and court review, all of which depend upon each person's values as they vote, adopt, and interpret the laws.

But we are not confined to responding with our initial thought or value. That is where the paradigm shift and choice come in. We may have our initial reaction to a situation, or core value. Maybe we have a prejudiced reaction when confronted with someone of another race, ethnicity, or lifestyle. This is where we get to pause and examine our value against the principle. Is our interpretation of the principle correct in this situation? Is our value in line with the principle or the ethic? If it is not, then we have the ability to respond how we choose, regardless of our first interpretation of the event. Yes, I am actually suggesting that you take time to think before you blurt out something really stupid or make a decision (remember we make choices) that you will regret.

Throughout history, people have talked about things like responsibility, compassion, fairness, and some form of citizenship or self-control as being principles. The Apostle Paul wrote about kindness and self-control in Galatians 5:23. Refer back to your best-leader list, and you will find these things are included in your requirements for a good leader.

We may hear people at work argue that they are fighting about principles. So how do we look at principles in an organization? We know principles involve things such as honesty, kindness, compassion, and fairness, and that those are also values. Which principle are you fighting for? Most of our time is spent fighting about preferences. What color they paint the company car is probably a preference. What time they want you at work may be just a preference. What color the uniforms are may be just a preference (unless this is based on a statutory requirement). Whether the company requires ties or long sleeves is just a preference. Let's explore something:

> A person at work has been accused of committing a policy violation, and the investigation shows that the person is guilty. The supervisor suggests a penalty of a one-day suspension without pay. The department head suggests a two-day suspension without pay. The division chief suggests a three-day suspension without pay. The regional manager insists on a four-day suspension without pay. What is the principle, and what is the preference?

Does the fact that the employee was convicted of the violation satisfy the principle? Is the amount of time of the suspension just a preference? What if someone else committed the same offense but received a different penalty? Would that make it a principle issue? Fairness seems to have been a principle-based value for most of the experts, but fairness is always something that varies greatly depending on the opinion or the paradigm of the individual. If the regional manager suggested a thirty-day suspension, that might be so unreasonable or excessive as to be a principle-based issue. If the differences in suggested penalties seemed to be based on race, ethnicity, or gender, that could make it a principle-based issue. Is the amount of the penalty always a preference?

Let's apply this to the enforcement of company policies. Everyone likes to get away with not having to comply with policies they don't agree with or are uncomfortable with. An example might be a policy that requires employees to wear ties, long-sleeve shirts, or business attire to any company gathering; one manager allows members of his unit to wear polo shirts or casual wear, while another manager forces his people to comply with the policy. This creates a problem of inconsistency. People may want to work for the manager who allows people to violate policy rather than the one who is strict on the rules. What happens when the regional director shows up and the lax manager's employees are all in violation?

Trust is an essential part of leadership, and for trust to exist, there must be consistency and predictability in the leader. Warren Bennis and Burt Nanus agreed in their book *Leaders*: "One thing we can say for sure about trust, for trust to be generated there must be predictability."[66]

Morale
People generally want to be held accountable, but they want everyone else to be held accountable also. A manager who is flexible on one policy may be flexible on other policies, but it all boils down to the manager doing what he wants at the time. When we find ourselves in a situation like that, we have no idea what policy will be enforced on any given day or if we will get in trouble at this manager's whim. Wishy-washiness has emerged!

---

[66] Bennis and Nanus, *Leaders*, 153.

These types of issues have a huge effect on morale and on people, quality, discipline, and productivity. If morale were just about happiness, then everyone would be happy with a polo shirt. We have mentioned this happiness thing before. Is it better to be liked or to be respected? What effect can this have on morale? I believe the formula for morale involves three elements: pride, professionalism, and productivity.

Pride is the element that the leader has the least control over, and that the group tends to build on itself. Let's go back to General Savage and *Twelve O'Clock High* for a moment. The 918th Bomb Group did not have much pride before General Savage came in; in fact they had a lot of self-pity and fear.

You can't demand the units have pride in themselves and the company. Savage demanded they show professionalism. We can equate professionalism to discipline. He made them follow the rules with no exceptions for anyone, including himself and his command staff. When you look at other good leaders, they all seem to have that in common. There was no confusion about which rule or policy applied on each day. It was always consistent; everyone knew exactly where they stood.

You can demand productivity. Savage did that by requiring everyone to perform to a high standard. Every good leader performs to their best and requires people to follow with their best performance.

Professionalism and productivity are things you have some control over. You can set a standard and demand that team members meet it or look for another line of work. Savage set those standards, and gradually the group accepted them. Eventually the group realized they had become a quality unit whose performance was nothing short of excellent. Pride in themselves, pride in the unit, and pride in each other began to rise as a result.

We showed this as three vials: pride, professionalism, and productivity. All the vials are connected and tend to leak. Because of human nature, we tend to slack off, if we are not led. Professionalism and productivity have wide openings that we can fill. Pride has a very narrow opening that is very difficult to fill except by praise for excellence, BLTs (bright lights and trumpets), and intrinsic rewards. The leader's job is to keep filling those vials.

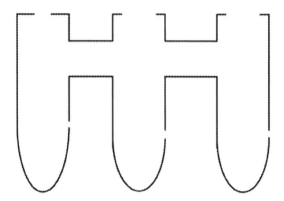

Pride + Professionalism + Productivity = Morale

Vision

In demanding productivity and professionalism, you may be met with some questions, lack of trust, and resistance unless you have established purpose and have created trust. Savage does that when he is talking with the pilot, Lieutenant Bishop. He is explaining the vision, mission, purpose, and reasons behind the need to perform at a maximum level. A leader provides the vision so that all can understand. *A leader inspires, animates, transforms purpose into action, creates determination, persistence, tenacity, and trust, and provides confidence for all involved.* Walt Disney said, "If you can dream it, you can do it."

The leader is responsible for communicating the vision and maintaining focus on that vision. The leader paints verbal pictures of the future state of the group. Savage told Bishop that "one day there will be a sea of bombers crossing the channel headed for Berlin." In 1983 Steve Jobs of Apple lured John Sculley from Pepsi to come to work as Apple's CEO by asking him if he wanted to sell soda all his life or change the world.

Leaders,[67] by Warren Bennis and Burt Nanus, was the seventh book in the program, selected to explore vision. "In the end," they wrote, "the

---

[67] Ibid.

leader may be the one who articulates the vision and gives it legitimacy, who expresses the vision in captivating rhetoric that fires the imagination and emotions of followers, which—through the vision—empowers other to make decisions that get things done."[68] They also said that all the leaders they used in their research seemed to be masters at selecting, synthesizing, and articulating an appropriate vision of the future. They said that they also learned it was a "common quality of leaders through the ages."[69]

Bennis and Nanus interviewed many leaders to write the book *Leaders*. It covers many of the same elements of leadership that we have been discussing. They make references to Pygmalion in empowering followers and discuss the importance of personal relationships, trust, and respect to leadership. They also begin with how important it is to work on and know yourself as a leader. They describe various organizational conditions and provide strategies for dealing with people and future forecasting for business.

Vision always refers to a future state of the organization. It is similar to the overarching goal from *Managing for Excellence*. Bradford and Cohen say that an overarching goal or vision should:

- reflect the core purpose of the department
- be feasible and obtainable;
- be challenging;
- and have a larger significance.[70]

Bennis and Nanus discuss how to develop a vision for the organization. They discuss looking at the past, present, and future for help with developing the vision. They provide some methodology to look at future trends using focus groups and brainstorming methods. They also talk about leaders who were good at taking chances on ideas and studying the past to help with development. One of the simplest ideas they have is just asking ourselves,

---

[68] Ibid., 109.
[69] Ibid., 101.
[70] Bradford and Cohen, *Managing for Excellence*, 103–5.

"What business are we in?" Drucker and other management theorists also shared that idea in early works. It sounds simple, but it is probably one of the most important questions we can ask. Examples would be Verizon or AT&T, two communications companies that have expanded into all forms of communications, not just phones.

Vision is the way for leaders to excite their followers and pull them along rather than push or force them. Once people are inspired and take on the vision, the leader may just need to get out of the way.

We see lots of examples out there today of companies who have broken the traditional management models, latched onto the vision of the leader, and become runaway successes, such as Yahoo, Apple, and Zappos. The employees are in sync with their leaders' vision and direction. Everyone has a shared purpose to push the vision forward. They all understand that the success of the company is their responsibility. There is no need for strict management, tough supervision, or a dress code. They are all committed to have pride and professionalism, and they create more productivity than the scale can measure. "Contemporary leadership texts make compelling arguments for leaders to drive fear out of organizations, to share power, to invite feedback and to encourage participation."[71]

In the 1970s, if you asked a janitor at NASA what he was doing, he would respond, "Sending a man to the moon and back." NASA's vision was to go "to the moon and back" (all the astronauts were glad it was not a one-way trip!). If you asked the POW's in Vietnam what their vision was, they would say it was "to return with honor." Organizations that share a common vision are tenacious and tough to stop.

Organizations should have a vision that is provided by leadership, but there are many levels of leadership in the organization. You may be the leader in your group, but report to other levels also. As part of the leadership you always have a part in the vision of the organization. You may not have created it, but you are part of it.

---

[71] Chaleff, Ira, *The Courageous Follower* (San Francisco, CA: Berrett-Koehler Publishing, 1995), 5.

An organization can have many different opinions, perspectives, and desires. Each area tends to want things done in a way that will benefit that particular area. In the police department we have many separate areas, groups, and teams, such as patrol, detectives, narcotics, vice, training, traffic, aero, personnel, administration, records, and so on. In business we have sales, shipping, receiving, marketing, manufacturing, research, development, administration, analysis, and so on, every one with their own perspective and ideas.

The leaders' job at all levels is to maintain focus on the vision despite the different perspectives. Without the leaders maintaining focus, we can have several different visions that take departments in different directions that do not support the mission and vision as defined by the organization. It goes along with the leader's ability to maintain discipline and order without having to force people to follow. It is also part of clearly establishing and communicating the standards and direction of the company or as Bennis and Nanus put it, the social architecture.

A student in the leadership program shared a story about his department's desire to develop a vision/mission statement. He saw this as an excellent chance to help establish a vision by which the department could develop a whole new mind-set. Like all departments, they had a huge policy and procedure manual that covered many things very specifically, but was impossible to memorize. He wanted to change the mind-set of the department and use the idea of honor from the Vietnam War POWs' "return with honor" motto as part of their mission statement. His thought was that if they could get buy-in from the entire department, there would not be as much need to rely only on that giant book of rules; everyone would do things based on an honor code, and there would be less misconduct.

His chief liked the idea. Upper management agreed that it was a good idea and took over creating a process to implement the program. They set out to notify the personnel of the new motto by memorandum. They had it printed boldly on department letterhead and distributed. They had it painted on the sides of the police cars and posted in the hallways.

This was not how he envisioned the implementation, however. He tried to explain they needed to create a plan that began with the first-line supervisors and develop a training program through which first-line supervisors (sergeants) would facilitate discussions about honor using all the methods we have discussed. The goal was to attack the department at a gut value level to understand the meaning of honor and how it played into the role of the police department and the community. They needed time to build the consensus for buy-in and a change in the culture of the organization. He felt there was a lack of understanding by management, as they failed to pursue a bottom-up process.

The result was that all those nicely printed declarations were found in the trash cans around the department. The painted motto on the sides of the cars was defaced by the officers. While management had the best intentions, the officers felt it was forced on them, and they never bought in.

This happens frequently in organizations of all kinds. Many managers read the material but fail to get to a deep understanding of what is being said. It goes back to *Zen and the Art of Motorcycle Maintenance* and understanding the underlying forms, not just the veneer, as well as to Kolb's *Adult Learning* and grasping and transforming into the aha experience.

I have said this a number of other ways, but here is how Bennis and Nanus say it: "All leaders face the challenge of overcoming resistance to change. Some try to do this by the simple exercise of power and control, but the effective leaders, learn that there are better ways to overcome resistance to change. This involves the achievement of voluntary commitment to shared values."[72]

How do we get voluntary commitment? Bennis and Nanus reinforce what we have discussed from "Zen and the Art of Management" and other earlier material. "The decision making style is participative and encourages a bottom-up flow of ideas aimed at generating consensus around all issues."[73] In other words, involve the members of the group in the process.

---

[72] Ibid., 185.
[73] Ibid., 120.

The leader can give the direction, the vision, and the mission, but all good leaders listen sincerely to and work *with* the members of the group.

One More Look at Ethics in Leadership

Leaders begins with what we began with; the authors call it "leading others and managing self." Bennis and Nanus and all the ninety leaders they studied in their book all talk about the need for the leader to have integrity, honesty, tenacity, good values, moral character, and humility. "The management of self is critical. Without it, leaders may do more harm than good. Like incompetent physicians, incompetent managers can make people sicker and less vital."[74] And on the concept of humility, they say, "There was no trace of self-worship or cockiness in our leaders."[75]

The Power of Ethical Management (1988) by Kenneth Blanchard and Norman Peale[76] is a short but worthwhile read that has some very simple guidelines for ethical behavior:

1. *Is it legal?* Does it violate company policy, or civil or criminal law? If it is not legal, we can stop right here; we need no further debate.
2. *Is it balanced?* Is it fair to all concerned, in the long and short term? Does it give me or someone else an unfair advantage?
3. *How will it make me feel about myself?* If it was reported on the TV news or the front page of the newspaper, would I be proud or would I be embarrassed? Does it violate my values?

Everyday Ethics,[77] by Joshua Halberstam, was the eighth book, used to explore ethics in this portion of the program. Halberstam covers practically everything: friends and foes, judging yourself and others, creeps and saints, sex and romance, talk and emotion, moral clichés, and a host of other topics. He discusses things I had never thought about, such as why

---

[74] Ibid., 56.

[75] Ibid., 57.

[76] Blanchard, Kenneth, and Peale, Norman, *The Power of Ethical Management* (New York: William Morrow, 1998).

[77] Halberstam, Joshua, *Everyday Ethics* (New York: Penguin Group Publishing, 1994).

we have friends that don't share our own value systems. I know some folks who have friends that they say are totally unethical, even criminal, but they still hang out with them. Halberstam makes us wonder why. We always want some diversity in our lives; it is not good to only be around people who agree with all of our political and social points of view. It is always good to look into other perspectives and ideas that will keep us constantly evaluating our own positions and paradigms. Hanging out with criminal minds may not be healthy though!

Ever since I read Halberstam's book, I see and hear things in very different ways. I recently heard our city council debating an ordinance that would ban registered sex offenders from our city parks where children play. Several members said they did not want to approve the ordinance because they had friends who were registered sex offenders; they were not sure they could support such an ordinance since their friends also had children of their own. I thought to myself, "That is so wrong on so many levels. Why would someone ever admit to that?" I had always thought that we sent people to the city council because they were pillars of the community, moral and trustworthy, but your friends can be an indication of your values.

In order to really learn about ethics, morals, and values, it is necessary to get into some discussion and view some scenarios or exercises. It is always interesting to see this turn into dialogue or a search for the truth. The dialogue begins to explore values and goes places where mortals fear to tread, "elephant talk" as Halberstam puts it. In my law enforcement class, I start off discussing something as simple as gratuities. Most agencies have rules against accepting gratuities for the reason that it tends to breed favoritism. If they give the cops something for free or half price, some parties will begin to feel like they owe something or they will expect something in return.

We explore this at length in class to try to see if it is wrong and why. I can tell you I have experienced the embarrassment firsthand: I am in a restaurant, in uniform, for my dinner break, and walk over to the counter to pay. The sixteen-year-old behind the counter yells across the room to the manager, "Hey, do we still give the cops half price?" Everyone in the place turns to look at me. I suddenly feel intimidated and embarrassed, and want to hide. There must be something wrong with this if I feel this way.

During class discussion, I would push deeper into dialogue, and one of the participants would often say, "It is a breach of our value system." They would go on to explain, "We have a value system. We don't lie, cheat, steal, or tolerate those who do. This makes us feel like we are getting something we don't deserve, and therefore it's as if we are stealing. That is why we feel like it is wrong and a violation of our integrity, selling out our honor for a lousy hamburger, cup of coffee, or whatever it might be." It takes us back to the question "How will it make me feel about myself?" This process of exploring through dialogue is adult learning and my suggestion as to how we learn about ethics—we talk to each other!

I also want to mention whistle blowers and the damage that can result from these actions. I like to review an article from *Harper's*, "The Case of the Corporate Coward: The Great Aircraft Brake Scandal."[78] This article tells about an engineer, working for the B. F. Goodrich Corporation on a project for the design and production of brakes for the A7D aircraft. The engineer repeatedly warned of design problems and brake testing that was falsified, but was ignored. Management was aware of the problems, but refused to acknowledge them and made every attempt to cover up the issue. Even though the brakes failed constantly in testing, the whistle-blowing engineer was the one singled out and punished. Nearly everyone else on the project was promoted or rewarded in some fashion.

While this may be the right thing to do, Lieutenant Cunningham warned that whistle blowing was like setting off a hand grenade in a crowded room; everyone will be injured, and it will get you also. This is another test of courage for leaders. It is essential that we do not let the little things go. When we are confronted with initial problems, we refuse to be party to them and we refuse to allow others to proceed. If you allow the little white lie, then you become a party to the crime.

---

[78] Vandivier, Kermit, "The Case of the Corporate Coward: The Great Aircraft Brake Scandal," *Harper's*, April 1972.

In class, we went through an exercise in which we imagined that we had been asked to falsify some statistics by the boss. Nearly everyone said they would not do what the boss had asked. Well, of course they would say that, since we had been talking ethics for six days of class. But how would this really play out? So, I ask them to commit to never knowingly allowing a false report to exist. Can I get you to commit to that also? It is easy to say this in class but a bit more difficult in real life. I finished off these sessions with an ethical dilemma:

I ask the group members to think about their two best friends in the police department, and then imagine that you are being assigned as the new Homicide Unit supervisor, where both of those friends are investigators working under you.

You recall a case where a three-year-old child was kidnapped, tortured, sexually assaulted, and murdered. The child's body was found with their mouth stuffed with dirty socks and wrapped with duct tape. You remember this case because before being assigned as the supervisor for the Homicide Unit you talked with your friends frequently about the investigation and how they were working to solve it. They did solve the case, and arrest and convict the killer, who confessed to everything. The killer has been sentenced, but appeals are pending.

After some time in your new assignment as the supervisor, you choose to review that case and sign out for the investigative files (also known as a murder book). While reading the case you begin to notice some details that don't match how the events were described to you earlier. It becomes increasingly clear to you that the investigators have lied about crucial parts of the investigation. You can also see that a sharp attorney could discover the discrepancies in the appeal process.

You know that if you bring this information forward, the murderer will, at minimum, get a new trial. Your friends will be investigated, as well as possibly fired and prosecuted, and could serve time in jail. Every case they have investigated in the past will be reviewed and possibly overturned. They will hate you, everyone in the department will hate you, and the reputation of the department will be severely damaged.

Since you have signed out for the murder book, you are now in the loop as far as evidence and testimony. If you are called to testify, you will need to lie to protect your friends. If you lie and become part of the conspiracy, you may end up in jail also.

There is no doubt that the murderer is guilty, but there is also no doubt the investigators falsified the report.

Do you know what the right thing to do is? Is doing it so wrong in other ways that it is just too difficult to choose a way out? That is what most ethical dilemmas are: choices between two right or two wrong situations, where there is just no clear way to solve the issue without incurring some damage.

Classes were usually very disturbed by this scenario. As we discussed this scenario in one particular class, the conversation took an unusual turn. This shift was led by one individual, who began to say that under no circumstances would he turn in the investigators. This person went further and said that whatever he, or any other "good cop," had to do to make sure the guilty party went to jail was okay.

As this discussion was going on, I noticed a female sergeant stand up from her table and lean against the wall. She was visibly upset and was obviously wrestling with the discussion. I watched her while I facilitated the discussion, and eventually asked if she had something to add.

She looked up with tears in her eyes and said that for years she had endured comments by people talking negatively about cops. She said people told her that cops lie, cheat, and steal property, drugs, and money from individuals. People had told her they had done drugs with officers, because "cops get the best dope." She would always answer that they were wrong. She would tell them that she worked with the best, most courageous people in the world. However, today she discovered she was wrong and they were right. She said she did not wish to be associated with the profession or the people in it any longer and was going back to her department to resign. She stormed out the door, sobbing.

I sent the auditors after her. It was so quiet that I thought everyone in the room had stopped breathing. Finally someone spoke up and said they should have spoken earlier to stop this nonsense. Then another person said they were ashamed they had not spoken up to stop the discussion from going the way it had. Eventually the class got into a deep dialogue about to why this was happening and why it was wrong. The entire group changed direction.

This one person chose to have the courage to speak and turn everything around. Her brave act saved a number of people from making huge misjudgments and mistakes. The group got an experiential learning session in group dynamics (one that was not supposed to happen until session six!).

I know I don't have all the answers to these things. I tell everyone that I surely don't want any of you opening my closet doors and letting those skeletons out, and I really don't want to open them myself. But, what we can do is choose now to start thinking about things in the ethical context that we will encounter as leaders. We cannot have a moral life at work and choose to live a different life at home or vice versa. We are what we are all day, every day, in every situation; we just have to choose what that will be. Do you have control over your actions? Do you have a choice as to which course you will take? Can you control your greed and your prejudice? Can you create trust, respect, inspiration, vision, and leadership?

Review and Evaluation

When I went through the program the first time, Cunningham had us write a midterm paper at this point. I thought I was a pretty ethical guy, but I was disturbed by some of my acts and my thoughts up to that point; I expressed that in my paper. I said I had been having a lot of fun up until then as a supervisor, but the thought that I had to be responsible for my acts and take action on the things I saw and all the things that I had knowledge of was disturbing. I felt like this was going to take some time to understand and sort out.

Cunningham's response was very compassionate; he wrote on a yellow Post-it note, "If you can't do the job, you should give up those sergeant stripes and get out of police work." After the initial shock wore off, I realized that was the best advice one leader could give to another.

Look for examples of values, ethics, and principles. Spend some time evaluating your behavior and the example you set for your friends and family. Think about the ethical messages you are sending to others. Examine your paradigm again based on your values and how they correlate to principles.

Look at your place in supporting or developing the vision in your organization. Meet with the boss to understand what the vision is and what you can do to help.

Make some midterm notes here describing how you have been affected by what you have learned so far.

Notes

Chapter Five

Keeping Myself in Line

I Don't Have Time for This

If you are doing it right, leadership is a time-consuming job. In most cases, doing things yourself assures that they are done quickly and correctly, right? Of course if you do it all yourself, you will never be able to go away on vacation or even retire. Time is one of the most valuable commodities we have in organizations, and learning how to use it is a necessary skill that all leaders and managers need. It is one of those teachable skills, but understanding how to delegate with the mind-set of the leader requires more thought. Leaders maintain a developer mind-set and will tend to use time differently than managers.

The ninth book we used in the leadership program was *Don't Do, Delegate,* by James M. Jenks and John M. Kelly.[79] Jenks and Kelly say that "delegation is the most important skill for a manager. In fact, it is the skill that defines the manager."[80] Knowing how and when to use it is one of the most important qualities for a leader. Jenks and Kelly say good managers "see subordinates as resources for achieving results. They help them make good use of their talents."[81] I think Jenks and Kelly are referring to using the team members' abilities to benefit the team and the overall results.

---

[79] Jenks, James M., and Kelly, John M., *Don't Do, Delegate* (New York: Ballantine Books, 1985).
[80] Ibid., 6.
[81] Ibid., 11.

Most of the book describes the managers' role in delegating to improve the managers' abilities and company efficiency; it also discusses development of employees and leadership thinking.

In class we had an "in basket" exercise that could represent a typical week at the office for most of us. We give the students a time limit to complete the exercise before they leave town for a week on an imaginary assignment. Afterward, we have them meet together to examine how they performed. We ask them to meet as a group and come to a consensus on the exercise. They are asked to describe how they prioritized things and what they learned. Since they have just read *Don't Do, Delegate,* it is an interesting exercise to see how and if they transformed the book into the mind-set of a developer and a leader.

In most cases, students tend to delegate to strengths. A team member who has similar skills will get assignments of a similar nature. The justification is always that, since we imposed a time limit on them, it was safer and easier to delegate to the strength.

In the exercise, team members must deal with a personnel matter, which they tend to delegate or simply postpone, because of limited time. They tend to ignore an inventory assignment, considering it not an important use of time, even though their boss will be blindsided when very crucial items are missing. They also place too much effort on a deployment assignment that is not time critical, but will be important several months in the future. They allow time to overpower the leadership mode and turn them into managers.

Jenks and Kelly make many good points about how to delegate. They specifically warn to use care in delegating personnel matters and confidential matters. They also encourage you to make your bosses look good; that means keeping them informed and not surprising them with missing inventory or information.

As leaders we should always look for opportunities to develop our people. We should delegate to weaknesses to improve abilities and train. We should delegate to increase confidence, responsibility, knowledge, and efficiency. We can always find an excuse (arguing for one's weaknesses) not to delegate properly. Proper delegation involves risk, personal involvement, patience, and more time than doing the task yourself would require. Many people miss how great the long-term rewards are when tasks are delegated properly.

We want to remember how we motivate, empower, and reward our followers. They are looking for challenges and, more important, trustworthy assignments; delegation is part of that process. In line with that idea, Jenks and Kelly discuss that proper delegation "always requires a certain degree of decision making on the circumstances," as well as "the authority and the other resources needed to complete the task."[82] In every task we delegate, we must also understand this is an adult learning experience. "The teacher in this process is not just the delegator, but the experience itself."[83]

We need to carefully select the people we delegate to. Admiral Rogge discussed this factor in selecting his officers and crew. Jenks and Kelly emphasize that "you cannot delegate effectively if you delegate arbitrarily. And, you cannot delegate effectively if you have only a superficial knowledge of your subordinates."[84]

You also cannot delegate and just walk away. It is going to require that you oversee the process to some degree. This is where all the previous time spent on communicating standards and expectations pays off. You must have developed a degree of trust with the person you have selected. As you delegate authority and decision making, you ask them to keep you informed of those actions they are taking. Jenks and Kelly talk about controls, and caution against too much or too little. The problem is that you do not want to be a micromanager, looking over everyone's shoulder, but you do want to impose timelines and goals so they will keep you informed.

---

[82] Ibid., 10–29.
[83] Ibid., 33.
[84] Ibid., 59.

We do not want to create the "Wallenda Factor" or the fear of failure. Karl Wallenda walked tightropes and fell to his death in 1978. His wife recalled that until three months prior to his accident, he had never thought of failure, but in the last three months, all he thought about was failing. Bennis and Nanus explain, "It became increasingly clear that when Karl Wallenda poured his energies into not failing rather than walking the tightrope, he was virtually destined to fail." They also reveal that the leaders they interviewed "simply don't think about 'failure', don't even use the word, relying on such synonyms as 'mistake', 'glitch', 'bungle' or countless others such as 'false starts', 'mess', 'hash', 'bollix', 'setback' and 'error'. Never failure."[85]

If we truly want to empower our employees, then we need to allow them to make mistakes within certain limits. "Mistakes," Jenks and Kelly explain, "aptly illustrate what not to do. And the person who has learned what not to do is wiser than the person who has never been allowed to venture far enough to make an error."[86] I believe that the leader should step in to prevent catastrophic errors, but if the potential error is something we can fix, we can chalk it up to learning. I would not allow them to injure others for the sake of a learning experience. What we are trying to do here is develop people capable of replacing us and excelling at it. We want to make ourselves dispensable. Most managers want to be indispensable to the company to assure themselves of a position, notice, promotion, and so forth; that is not the leader's mind-set. In a leader, success ensues and is not pursued, remember?

We are looking for time to develop people and still get the job done. Dr. Steven R. Covey suggests a great tool for time management, his time management matrix.[87]

---

85 Bennis and Nanus, *Leaders* (New York: Harper and Row, 1985), 69,70.
86 Jenks and Kelly, *Don't Do, Delegate*, 76.
87 Covey, Stephen R., *The 7 Habits of Highly Effective People*, 146–156.

	Urgent	Non-Urgent
Important	Quadrant 1	Quadrant 2
Non-Important	Quadrant 3	Quadrant 4

Covey's Time Management Matrix
The 7 Habits of Highly Effective People
Reprinted with permission

We cannot avoid time spent on true crisis, the urgent and important tasks (quadrant one). In reality, there is not much time spent in this area of true crisis. We spend little time dealing with tasks that are not urgent or important (quadrant four), primarily because they are not time driven. We tend to forget them or delegate them just to get rid of them. We tend to spend most of our time on tasks that are urgent but not really important (quadrant three). We might refer to this as "putting out brushfires." These events take time out of our day, create stress, and get in the way of our mission as leaders. So, where should we be spending time as leaders and developers?

In the developer mode, we do not need to be in a hurry. We have the ability to choose to operate in an area that is not urgent but is very important (quadrant two), to develop the future leaders and managers in the organization. The developer mind-set makes this area a priority and is always thinking about and looking for a way to develop people. The more we develop people, the less time we will spend in crisis and the less time we will spend putting out brushfires.

While operating in the developer mind-set, we can work on things such as vision building, focus, discipline, values, communication, skills, goal setting, team building, and empowerment, all leadership traits that we have discussed and need to focus on. Delegating to weaknesses that provide personal growth is important but not urgent (quadrant two).

As a leader you cannot be tied to your job. You need to be a leader in other areas of your life also. Leadership requires a balance of your time, or you will wear yourself out. You may be thinking, "You have no idea what my life is like: my boss, my job, my kids, and my spouse." You are right; I don't. But I'm not really into excuses, so get control of the things you do have control over and fix them! Think about your lifetime goal-setting exercise, and remember what is important. Even Dr. Covey says we have to learn to say no. If we want to find time to work in quadrant two, we need to eliminate some things, but they can't be things from quadrant one. There are ways to politely say no, such as, "I see how important that project is; however, I have a great deal of work here. Which task would you like me to delay to take time for this?"

You must also refuse to allow people to put monkeys on your back. Those are the people who come to you and suggest a project for you to do. You should politely say, "That is a great idea; I think you can handle that. Keep me informed of your progress." If you really do not want to be disturbed, use the universal sign and close your door!

Dr. Covey refers to two types of delegation: gofer delegation and steward delegation.[88] Gofer delegation is just what it sounds like: assigning to other people the tasks you don't want to do. Steward delegation is developing people. As a leader, how would you handle gofer delegation? Should that need to be delegated in the first place?

When you tackle your in basket, approach it in this manner: Each time you pick up a piece of paper place a dot in the upper left-hand corner (mark emails read or create a folder). When it has three dots in the corner (or three reviews), you need to reevaluate whether or not the task associated with that communication should be your job. In all likelihood, it should be

---

88 Ibid., 173–4.

someone else's job, so transfer that assignment to the person or place it belongs. General Robert E. Lee prided himself on having a clean desk. He thought that allowed him to concentrate his efforts on development and strategy. Delegate as a developer—always! Review everything, prioritize everything, and reassign work and responsibility to the level at which it should be.

Jenks and Kelly suggest that policy is something that should not be delegated, but I have found that delegating policy can be very rewarding if done properly. If the team members are making policy, they will feel ownership of the policy and of the management. They will share in management and leadership, developing true shared values in the organization. It also gives them areas to present for promotional opportunity. They can demonstrate the ability to be part of management/leadership in the organization by showing the ability to complete staff work and upper management responsibilities. It is a huge trust-building block.

I had an officer who felt badly about an event that had occurred as a result of our policy for handling intersections where the traffic signals were out due to power failures. There were many legal issues involved, and the city attorney's position was that the police should not direct traffic under those circumstances, as it made the city liable for any accidents. If we did not control the intersection, we had no liability. The officer felt we had a moral obligation to the public to control the intersection, so I gave him the responsibility of rewriting the policy. He put a tremendous amount of effort and research into the revision, while keeping up his regular assignments. He got input from other officers and supervisors as well as legal opinions and traffic engineering advice.

The resulting policy was excellent and received immediate department-wide buy-in. It changed his perspective on many things and was very useful to him in being promoted to supervisor.

What Is Your Motive?
We need to spend some time talking about people's motives. We have discussed the mind-set of the leader, but people can be difficult. Let's look

at undermining first. In class we used the movie *Tunes of Glory*[89] as a case study for this dynamic.

Tunes of Glory is an older movie (adapted from the novel and screenplay by James Kennaway) about a post-WWII Scottish brigade that is expecting a new commander. The acting commander is Jock Sinclair. Sinclair came up through the ranks and is a tough officer who really thrives on cronyism. He desires the command and feels that, by all rights, it should be his. But because of past behavior, headquarters has passed him over and is sending a new commander, Colonel Basil Barrows. Barrows is an officer who was brought up through the academy, with limited combat experience, but was also a prisoner of war, who bears some psychological scars from that experience.

Sinclair sets out on a mission to undermine and embarrass the new commander. He proves to be very effective at this, destroying Barrows and himself and causing tremendous damage to the brigade. Both John Mills (playing Colonel Basil Barrows) and Alec Guinness (playing Major Jock Sinclair) received British film award nominations for best actor. The film was also nominated for best picture, received an Academy Award nomination for best screenplay, and won the Hollywood Free Press award for Best Foreign Film.

There are many examples in this movie of motive, undermining, and the destructive results of such actions for leadership in an organization. As leaders we know there will be people out there who will undermine us. We also know exactly how to undermine others. There is always a motive in undermining. Undermining is always done for personal gain. Take a few minutes to think about how we undermine others and how people undermine us. There is no doubt that you have experienced another supervisor or manager who has undermined you to make himself or herself look better. This behavior is especially vicious during promotional opportunities, competitions, and social events. People tend to rationalize the behavior at these times because it is a competition or an event, not work.

---

[89] *Tunes of Glory*, United Artists, 1969.

We need to understand that leaders do not engage in this behavior. Employees are not stupid, and they notice when the larger animals are fighting. It causes them to lose respect and trust in leadership as they immediately see that it has become about selfishness. When leaders undermine each other, it causes decay in discipline and the overall effectiveness of the entire organization.

Supportive confrontation is not undermining. If you take your grievances to someone in a manner that is meant to help, that is courage. Talking behind someone's back, whining, complaining, and cynical behavior are undermining.

Ira Chaleff wrote *The Courageous Follower*,[90] the tenth book used in the program and an excellent model for how to operate in a leadership environment. All of us as leaders have flaws and weaknesses. Chaleff describes the ways we should support each other as leaders and followers. As with most other leadership works, Chaleff talks about the importance of understanding ourselves and figuring out how we fit into the larger picture. "First we must understand our own power and how to use it. Second, we must appreciate the value of leaders and cherish the critical contributions they make to our endeavors. And, third, we must understand the seductiveness and pitfalls of the power of leadership."[91]

It is the pitfalls and the power of leadership that can lead to undermining. Undermining is not necessarily an action; inaction or allowing the leader to fail while you watch is also undermining. *Schadenfreude* is a German term for which there is no simple interpretation; it is that happy feeling you get when you are enjoying watching another person fail. While that may be acceptable in football, it is unacceptable in a leadership-based environment. Chaleff explains, "We have the right to challenge policies in the policy making process, we do not have the right to sabotage them in the implementation phase. It is our responsibility to give the policy a chance to make it work through energetic and intelligent adaptation rather than allow it to fail through literal interpretation or lukewarm execution.

---

[90] Chaleff, Ira, *The Courageous Follower*.
[91] Ibid., 3.

Each of us has the right to become an opponent. But if we do so covertly, without declaring our opposition, while still holding our position and demeanor as a follower, we create havoc within the organization."[92]

I am sure many of us have been undermined by other supervisors or managers, or even by our leaders at some time. Supervisor shopping occurs when things like this happen. It breaks down the discipline of the organization on a number of levels. It is how weak leaders make people like them—by giving them what they want when others will not.

I worked with another manager who had really endeared himself to his troops. He did this by constantly violating the rules and allowing indiscriminate violations of policy to go unchecked. On occasion, we would have to cover a shift for this manager, and it was always a disaster. He would leave the shift short, below minimum staffing levels, because he generously granted time off (probably knowing he would not be there to deal with the fallout anyway). As a result, whoever covered the watch would be forced to order people in from home or hold people over to meet required minimum staffing. This always made someone else out to be the bad guy. The officers did not understand that it was the manager's fault for allowing the time off to go uncovered. Even when another supervisor had previously denied time-off requests, this particular manager would approve them at a later date. It created a poor working environment for everyone.

While we quite often get undermined by someone above us in management, this is no excuse to undermine others. Courage requires that we confront the problem in a constructive manner. Even though we do not have control over what the boss does, we do have control over what we do. In order to keep things working smoothly, it is necessary to cover the weaknesses of the boss. Chaleff covers that over and over in his work. Undermining is never acceptable behavior for a leader.

Cynical behavior, as demonstrated through our actions or the actions of others, is another element we will deal with. Cynics have been around a long

[92] Ibid., 95.

time. The term actually emerged after the death of Socrates (Remember him from our discussion of Plato and ignorance as arrogance?). After Socrates' death, his followers split into several groups, including Sophists, Cynics, Hedonists, and Stoics. Cynics were like the Eeyores of old, walking the streets with the "it ain't ever gonna work," antiestablishment attitude.

I refer to cynics as people who are scornful of the motives of others, but offer no real options or help. They are typically bright, intelligent, quick witted, and experienced; but they will detract from the discussion or task. They will not take a stance on an issue but will shoot down other ideas. They are poor leaders but prove really effective at wreaking havoc and chaos. They usually know exactly what they are doing but sometimes act without thinking. A cynic typically makes a comment such as, "Let's get real here," or cracks a joke at someone else's expense to stop a conversation from approaching a very sensitive topic. This will defuse a situation when it gets too close or uncomfortable for him or her. They will justify this behavior as just being funny, but they can effectively kill off a discussion or progress towards a solution. They want to be seen as informal leaders, but they are actually cowards who refuse to accept responsibility or a real leadership role.

Now if that describes you, we really need to talk, because I believe it is necessary, for the good of the organization and the team, to kill a cynic. I don't mean physically, of course, but I do mean dethroning the individual. They can do irreparable damage to the organization, much like a cancer growing in your body.

In all the classes I facilitated, I learned that if I had one or two cynics, I could deal with them, and the class would eventually kill them. But if we had three, four, or more, it was a lost cause; the group would not go after them. Cynics are bright, and most people are afraid to challenge them because a good cynic can really make you look stupid or naive. Cynics can steal your power with the group and your ability to lead.

There are two things you should keep in mind with cynics. The first is that you must destroy this behavior. Don't try to take them on in a battle of wits in front of the group. Instead, give them the one thing they do not want, responsibility. Put them in charge of a task and give them plenty of leeway to work it out. You can give them that assignment in front of the group, being careful not to make it appear to be a vindictive act. Say something like, "It sounds like you may have a good idea of what is needed (or not needed) here, so please see me in the office and we can work out the details of your new assignment." Also, give them goals and timelines and hold them accountable. One of two things will happen; either they will become empowered since you have given them an opportunity to shine, or they will resist and eliminate themselves from the group through progressive punitive action.

The second thing to keep in mind about cynics is that you must search your heart and make sure that you are not one. Take some time to watch your comments, actions, and thoughts to review your own motives and choose to eliminate that demon from your character. Choose to change that paradigm without the need for a significant emotional event with the Sundance Kid.

We looked at this through another movie, *The Caine Mutiny*.[93] One of the officers in the film, Lieutenant Tom Keefer is the epitome of a cynic in this film adaptation of the book by Herman Wouk. We watch this movie to look at a number of issues: the role of a cynic, how to deal with a cynic, discipline in the organization, followers' responsibilities to support their leaders, how to deal with a difficult boss, and how to confront a boss.

The fictional movie follows life on board a US Navy destroyer minesweeper, the *USS Caine*, during WWII. Lieutenant Commander Queeg (the new captain) takes command of the ship from Lieutenant Commander DeVriess early in the movie. The movie details incident after incident of poor leadership and questionable behavior by Queeg.

During the movie, the officers have serious questions about the captain's actions during a combat engagement. Captain Queeg (Humphrey Bogart)

---

93 *The Caine Mutiny*, Columbia Pictures, 1954.

calls a meeting of the officers following this incident, and Lieutenant Keefer (Fred MacMurray) is also present. The captain is very disturbed by his own actions and is coming to the officers to ask for their help and support.

This is a very important moment in the development of courageous followership on board the *Caine*. In this incident, the captain offers an apology and asks for help before he exits and leaves the officers. Lieutenant Maryk, the executive officer (second in command), recognizes Queeg's humility, as do many other officers, who ponder the incident in silence; but our cynic, Lieutenant Keefer, breaks the silence with a funny comment. "This is what we refer to in literature as the pregnant pause," he says, offering just enough to break the tension of the moment and send everyone off without approaching the really important matter at hand.

More incidents occur, increasing the tension aboard the vessel until, during a typhoon, Lieutenant Maryk finally relieves Queeg of command to prevent the ship from sinking. Afterward Maryk and Ensign Keith (the officer of the deck at the time) are placed on trial for mutiny.

After Maryk and Keith's trial and subsequent acquittal, their attorney, Barney Greenwald, goes into a detailed examination of how they all failed in their leadership positions aboard the *Caine*. He cites the incident in which the captain came to the officers for help and they refused. He describes how the actions they took undermined the captain and discipline aboard the vessel. He asks whether they would have needed to take over during the typhoon, if they had done their jobs and been supportive of the captain. The officers start to take a look at themselves and their actions, which causes a paradigm shift and the realization they may actually have been guilty and failed in their duty.

Most people watch this movie seeing only a crazy captain who rolls steel balls in one hand when he gets stressed, or they remember it for the mad hunt for the missing strawberries. However, this movie is the perfect vehicle to explore the concept of being a courageous follower, understanding your role in leadership within an organization, and the necessity for courage and supportive confrontation.

Courage and Supportive Confrontation

When we think about courage, we usually associate it with some very physically dangerous act, such as charging up the hill under fire. Most would say that courage implies there is some risk associated with the act; if there is no risk, these people would argue, then it does not take courage. I believe that courage is an action taken based on values regardless of the consequences. Taking an action that is based on your value system and that you believe to be the correct course, no matter what will happen to you for sticking to your values, no matter the consequences, is a demonstration of courage.

I believe that would be consistent with the idea that courage involves risk. It can be as simple as confronting someone who is cheating or as dramatic as running into a burning building to save a life. While silence may be the safer choice, confronting the cheater is a value-based act if you believe in honesty and fairness. Chaleff has a great quote for this, "An individual who is not afraid to act on the truth as they perceive it, despite external inequities in a relationship, is a force to be reckoned with."[94]

The way many things go badly is that people choose the safety of being quiet instead of having the courage to speak up. This is something drilled into us as pilots. If you are a crew member, it is your duty to speak up and prevent the pilot from taking actions contrary to the safety of the aircraft and the souls on board. There are examples of crews not taking actions to prevent disaster, but most are recovered on the black-box recordings found in the wreckage.

We have a responsibility to keep our leaders informed, just as we expect to be kept informed as leaders. We need to hear all the options to be able to choose correctly, and we need people who are courageous and not afraid to tell us when things are going badly. Chaleff insists, "We should never protect a leader from bad news as it is an important source of feedback."[95] And we as leaders should demand that people have the courage to provide dissent. As long as our people are not afraid to provide dissent, we will

---

[94] Chaleff, Ira, *The Courageous Follower*, 18.
[95] Ibid., 59.

be able to maintain a perspective on options; it allows us to maintain a reality check. This is going to require a trust relationship between leaders and followers.

In providing or receiving information it is important to check the facts. Our "in basket" exercise included an anonymous rumor of sexual harassment. Quite often groups will key into that to create department-wide mandated training in sexual harassment policies, and start inquiries and investigations based on rumors. Pygmalion can be brought into action in such an instance, creating a self-fulfilling prophecy. When you hear about or see something, look into it; check the facts before you create a problem that does not exist.

Providing proper feedback is a good thing. It is a basis for building trust and power, whether you are the leader or the follower. As trust and power grow, you may get more feedback, or the leader may welcome more feedback and opinions from the followers. Chaleff warns, "Challenging a specific leader on a specific subject may be healthy, but a pattern of challenging all leaders on all subjects is not. A rebellious alienated follower will never earn the trust to meaningfully influence a leader."[96] It may be similar to our consideration of the tattletale versus the code of silence. We do not expect a code of silence, we want misconduct brought to light, but we do not want tattletales running around. I believe the difference lies in the motive of the tattletale, which is similar to that of the underminer. The motive is to make the tattletale look good at the expense of someone else, just like the motive of undermining is for personal gain.

Had the officers of the *Caine* been supportive of the captain and built a trust relationship among members of the group, things might have been completely different. The courage to challenge the leader in a reasonable manner is essential, and the leader needs to invite such challenges. We all know there are bosses who are not interested in our opinions, or at least that is what we think. You never really know how the boss will react until you take the time to give the boss a chance. It may be your perception

---

[96] Ibid., 37.

that the boss is not interested, or it may be your approach that causes the problem. Most bosses are very interested in making the organization work better and more efficiently. Any confrontation with the boss should be done in private, and the comments should be presented in a manner that is for the good of the organization.

Had the officers of the *Caine* supported the captain in his attempts to improve discipline and performance aboard the ship, they might have been able to establish a relationship of trust with the captain that would allow their concerns to be heard and taken to heart. I refer to this as supportive confrontation. It is letting the boss know that everything you do is in support of the purpose of the organization and part of an effort to improve overall efficiency. It is also providing feedback in an appropriate manner when you disagree with the direction or actions taken. Consider tempering the feedback as we discussed previously in chapter 3.

Supportive confrontation can take many forms. It is always something that is done only for the good of all concerned and is never done with a selfish motive. Supportive confrontation is the same thing you do with a good friend who is making a mistake in his or her life (such as abusing drugs or alcohol, mishandling finances, or having an affair). You should be telling this person that he or she is making a mistake rather than standing by and watching the meltdown. Leaders accept and use this concept both personally and professionally.

I tried to be a good leader and practice what I preached; but none of us is perfect. We all experience moments of weakness that require the support of our friends to keep things in the proper perspective. While I was managing the aviation unit, I developed a good trust relationship with my team. I was a team member as well as the leader. One afternoon, I met with a woman on a project and invited her out to the heliport for a tour. After she left, one of my pilots came into my office, sat down on the couch, looked at me, and just asked, "What are you doing?" I was a little taken aback by his comment but asked, "What do you mean?" He said, "Boss, that looks like trouble. Are you sure you want to go there?" I knew he loved me as much as I loved him, and I was not offended at his assumption. He was taking a risk to put my best interest ahead of his own. Friends are not afraid to confront each other in love and support to prevent or correct mistakes whether they are personal or professional.

In the early days of the leadership institute, the instructor meetings could be quite contentious. We were not afraid to confront each other about our teaching methods, subject matter, motives, and so on. We had a small group of instructors (about ten), and we were all committed to excellence. We left our egos outside (sometimes) and just tried to make the best program we could. Sometimes, finding out you are wrong is painful and uncomfortable, but knowing that criticism has been offered out of love sure makes it much more bearable.

Discipline

In *The Caine Mutiny*, discipline aboard the ship is pretty lax. As the movie begins, Captain DeVriess is in charge. On Ensign Keith's initial arrival aboard the *Caine*, he is immediately shocked at the lack of discipline and the condition of the vessel. His hope is that discipline will be restored upon the arrival of the new commander, who turns out to be Captain Queeg. Sometimes, you need to be careful what you wish for; what Keith got was another extreme.

Discipline is a very necessary part of any organization. It is an essential part of leadership. It is a method for communicating the values of the organization and the leader. For our purposes here, *discipline* is not the same as punishment. Discipline is derived from *disciple* and means someone who is part of an order or course of study, things such as martial arts, a particular teaching, a field of study, or a prescribed behavior. Most people use the term *discipline* to mean correcting people or forcing someone to maintain a standard or order, as in "he was disciplined for the error," but I am going to refer to that as punishment. Punishment is what we get for failing to maintain discipline.

Can you see discipline? When you see someone, meet someone, see a program, read a book, or see a movie, you are evaluating it against your paradigm. When you arrive for a new job you are evaluating the people, the environment, and the bosses. First impressions are extremely important. It is why we want police officers to look sharp; it communicates a sense of discipline, authority, and professionalism that instills confidence and trust. It is why one organization may demand a professional look while another organization does not; in either case, they are communicating values.

Command Sergeant Major John M. Stevens wrote a couple of articles I like to use, "First Impressions" and "Combat Ready."[97] While CSM Stevens writes for the military, his comments apply to any and all organizations. He says, "There are many ways to identify whether or not an organization cares for its soldiers. The introduction of the immediate supervisor and the immediate establishment of the 'you belong' relationship with the crew or squad are musts." He also discusses the immediate assignment of a bunk and a wall locker, which correspond to work space, offices, lockers, break room areas, and so on, in an office setting.

CSM Stevens is referring to a new employee coming into your organization and the values you will communicate to him or her upon entering. Are new hires going to look at the organization as being unorganized, not prepared for them, or unwelcoming? Or will they immediately feel and think, "This place has its act together, so I need to step up and be part of that?" This is the crucial time when we get to set the tone for our team members; they are going to get a dose of the ethical and professional environment we expect them to be an integral part of.

Discipline is a method to reduce anxiety and build trust and confidence. CSM Stevens says. "Long hours of training must do more than produce a trained platoon. They must create confidence in each crewman. … Mutual confidence and belief will only materialize if every soldier feels like a part of the platoon." He is telling us that, if we have the confidence in everyone to do their job and do it correctly, we can relax and concentrate on doing ours to the best of our ability. It is part of the team-building process we discussed in our look at *Managing for Excellence*; discipline is a necessary

---

[97] Command Sergeant Major Stevens, John M., *First Impressions from Armor*, November–December 1983 9, 85 (FC 22-4)-1198, *Combat Ready from Armor*, January–February 1984, 7, 85(FC 22-4)-1198.

part of team building. While this is extremely important in combat, it is equally important in business. We must know that everyone knows how to do his or her job and can be counted on to do it correctly. Discipline aids us in the predictability that provides trust and confidence to everyone.

If we look at an organization like Zappos or Microsoft, there is no value placed on the way people dress or neatness in the workplace. However, there is value placed on performance and creativity, and that discipline is communicated very well in those organizations. There is value placed on the comfort and care of each employee, and therefore the organizations are very disciplined.

The concept of showing that we care for our employees is very crucial. We have discussed this in many parts of this book. Since we discussed *The Caine Mutiny,* I wanted to add a note here about mutiny, votes of no confidence, and the like. What is the tipping point that causes mutiny? Is it too much demand for order and discipline? Is it enforcing rules, morals, and ethics? Is it refusing to grant vacation and leave time, cutting down lunch breaks, poor morale, and unhappiness? These are all valid problems, but those things can exist in many organizations that continue to function. I think the tipping point is when team members come to realize their leader does not care for them and would sacrifice them in a heartbeat for the leaders' own advancement. Even Machiavelli warned us a thousand years ago that we can make people fear us, but we cannot endure hatred. Do you feel discipline is an essential element in your life?

Duty, Honor, Country

This section was originally meant for government officials, police officers, members of the military, and anyone who takes an oath of office; however, it is an essential part of leadership for everyone to understand the values associated with duty, honor, and country conflicts. They are conflicts we have in everyday life, as well as in all professions, which go to the core values of loyalty, honor, and integrity.

Place yourself as an observer in the cockpit of a B-2 Stealth Bomber, streaking across the ocean headed for Russia on a bomb mission. You have nuclear weapons on board and targets that include heavily populated civilian areas. The orders are clear, and there is no mistake. You are only minutes away from killing many thousands of people, and the tension is so thick you can cut it with a knife. Suddenly, the pilot says that he just cannot do it. He refuses to carry out the mission and disengages the autopilot to turn the plane around. The copilot draws a weapon, orders the pilot to return to course and carry out the mission—or the copilot will shoot him. The copilot is forced to shoot the pilot to regain control of the aircraft and continue the mission. A few minutes later, the aircraft and mission are recalled, and you all return to base. What will happen to the copilot?

The copilot was carrying out his sworn duty, and the pilot was refusing to complete his sworn duty. Is the copilot guilty of anything? Both of them swore an oath to protect and defend the United States from all enemies and support the Constitution. They are officers and are therefore duty-bound to carry out all legal orders. Is the copilot duty-bound to complete the mission even if it means shooting the pilot to accomplish it?

Such an order, such responsibility, and such stress are almost unimaginable for most of us, but we live with this possibility every day, unconscious of the threat. We may not be the ones who turn the launch key or press the button, but we are all part of this as a society and may be on the sending or receiving end of this at any time. It is an issue we should consider every time we cast a ballot, take on a government contract, or work for the development of technology that makes this possible.

Our government and military officials all take oaths of office, but what exactly does that mean? Does it mean the oath taker can choose any action or quit anytime he or she wants? If that is the case, then what good is taking an oath? If I get a job or task I don't want to do, why can't I just quit and walk away just like someone who sells shoes? After all, if I don't like smelling dirty feet, I can just quit. Why is a sworn official any different? What is an oath anyway? Is it merely a contract? Many companies require employees to sign contracts to maintain confidentiality with respect to trade secrets, formulas, and technologies. Is an oath any different?

Robert E. Lee described an oath as a promise I make to myself that, no matter what happens, I will do as the oath prescribes. That was an issue for him as he wrestled with his oath to the United States of America and chose to lead the Army of Virginia during the Civil War. He may have rationalized his choice in saying that he swore the oath to his country and he saw his country as Virginia, which was being attacked by the States of the North. Hitler's generals tried to assassinate him, but they also wrestled with their oaths and whether they could carry out such an act of treason.

It would appear that the oath takes away some ability to choose what you will support and what you won't. If it is a law, then you are required to support that law until such a time as it is changed or declared unconstitutional by the courts. You are welcome to disagree with the law, but you are bound by duty if you have sworn an oath to uphold the law. This likely presents difficult choices for politicians and people in certain positions such as the attorney general.

In California, peace officers have discretion on many things, but in domestic violence cases the discretion is taken away by law. If there is probable cause to believe a crime has been committed, the officers on the scene must make an arrest. Failure to act is a punishable offense; failing to act is a violation of duty and the sworn oath.

Most people never really understand or realize the potential weight of that oath. To explore this more deeply, we separate the values: duty relates to organizational values, honor is considered a personal value, and country is thought of as the community's values. We want to bring this to the forefront and wrestle with the conflicts between values, so we used the movie *Billy Budd*[98] based on the novel by Herman Melville.

Billy Budd (played by Terrance Stamp) is a young seaman who is impressed into service in 1797 on a British man-of-war vessel during war with the French. The law gave a British commander the right to impress seaman into duty in the king's navy. He was taken off a merchant ship named *The*

---

[98] *Billy Budd*, Allied Artists, 1962.

Rights of Man, and on board the HMS *Avenger,* Billy is quickly assimilated into the crew. He performs admirably, obtaining promotion to foreman of the maintop, a leadership position on a crew that attends to the sails.

Billy is a really nice kid, a little naive and a little slow or mentally challenged. The master at arms is Mr. Claggart (Robert Ryan), a mean-spirited, evil man whose desire is that Billy be punished and broken for little more than Claggart's own amusement. When Claggart's attempts to frame Billy fail, he makes up a charge of mutiny and accuses Billy in front of Captain Veer (played by Peter Ustinov). Billy is innocent, but is overcome with anger and strikes out, hitting Claggart. Claggart loses his footing from the battery, falls, and strikes his head and dies. The Captain is forced by law to convene a court-martial and try Billy. The punishment for striking an officer, regardless of cause, is death by hanging. The court-martial must decide a verdict and a punishment.

This dilemma was played out in class as we paused the film and debated the case. It raised some real issues as the values of duty, honor, and country collide in a decision-making process that may take Billy's life. If you put yourself in the seat of the decision makers, is there any way to save Billy and still do your duty as prescribed by law? The arguments are sincere and the choices difficult. Should you choose to save Billy, you place yourself squarely in the position of treason, thereby condemning yourself to the very justice you seek to protect Billy from. What is the right thing to do, and do you have a choice? I have had people so disturbed by the choice in this section that they will call me and the other students at home in the month between sessions to discuss it and continue to debate the options.

Duty, honor, and country values often come into conflict in day-to-day situations. We see these conflicts continually as we are stressed to carry out the mission of a company that rubs against the grain of our personal value. There are conflicts that arise because we are placed in a situation where we really feel an act is wrong, but the company demands it and the community supports it. Think back to General Savage in *Twelve O'Clock High*; his conflicts in completing the missions clashed with how much he cared for the men he was sending into combat.

Lieutenant Colonel Zeb B. Bradford Jr. described this in an article titled "Duty, Honor and Country vs. Moral Conviction."[99] According to Bradford, "Fortunate is he whose principles and interests coincide. Fortunate especially is the soldier who serves a government which has moral integrity." This should be easy for you to equate to the corporate world, your political views, and your personal life as well. If the company is acting unethically or illegally, do you continue to support those values? Do you vote party lines or your own convictions? If your spouse, child, or other relative is committing crimes, is it a matter of honor to support them or the law? Colonel Bradford is saying that we are fortunate to be in an organization in which we all share values.

Laws get changed because the community no longer supports them due to a change in personal values. That is still the process in our society today. When I first went to work as a police officer, possession of one marijuana seed would send you to state prison. Now, you can legally sell a handful of medical marijuana seeds for thousands of dollars. We have made some adjustment to the letter of the law in our society. The California Penal Code clearly states we are to enforce the spirit of the law rather than just the letter of the law.

We are supposed to use reason to interpret the spirit of the law, as in reasonable cause, reasonable search and seizure, or beyond a reasonable doubt. If you are going to be a leader, then reason and fairness are values you will need to have onboard, as well as an understanding of duty. Leaders are required to balance these values to be fair. If you watch *Billy Budd*, you will discover just how difficult that can be. Duty cannot always prevail; it must be balanced with courage, honor, country, and tempered by moral conviction.

Review and Evaluation

The beauty of looking at these movies and reading the suggested books is that it helps you begin to get a real understanding of what all of this entails. There are so many little connections, actions, interpretations, and events

---

[99] Lesson 5, Leadership, What a Leader Must Do L5-AS-1-1. Lt. Col. Bradford, Zeb B., Jr., "Duty, Honor, and Country vs. Moral Conviction," *Army Magazine*, September 1968, 42–4.

that help to form that aha experience; it just can't be explained fully in this book (otherwise it would be the size of the national budget). I encourage you to take a time out and watch the movies as you read this book.

For this section I would like you to concentrate on situations that involve undermining and cynical behavior, specifically, how they affect discipline in the organization or in your home. Undermining can occur between parents and create cynical behavior and disciplinary issues with children, so don't just look at this as a work-related issue. Do the same with delegation. Practice it in your family setting, allowing others to accept and grow with more responsibilities.

And lastly, evaluate what kind of friend you are to your spouse, your boss, and your kids. Are you a courageous follower or a leader who invites courageous followers' input?

I had a student in a class who shared that he was arguing with his boss over a deployment issue. He said he was really going at it with his boss, but the boss would not change his mind on the issue. Finally he told his boss that he could not understand why he didn't see his point of view, especially since he (the boss) was a graduate of the same leadership program. His boss said, "Why do you think I am letting you talk to me this way?"

Bang! Dang that Sundance Kid!

Notes

Chapter Six

Keeping the Group in Line

Do you still have all those balls in the air? I have given you lots of things to think about while you are trying to lead. Leaders continually think and assess themselves and their paradigms. Let's look at applying this to group dynamics while we maintain our look at the whole.

Group Dynamics

Have you ever done something you really didn't want to do, just because everyone else seemed to want to do it? Then once it was over, did everyone laugh about how they never really wanted to do it either but went along because they thought everyone else did? No one wanted to do it, but everyone did it anyway. Sound like madness? Professor Jerry B. Harvey, a management expert, did studies on this phenomenon and called it the "Abilene Paradox." It exists when a group collectively agrees to do something that is really counter to the desires of any of the members. CRM did a training video on this phenomenon, *The Abilene Paradox, the Management of Agreement.*[100]

The fable that gives the phenomenon its name tells of a family taking a fifty-three-mile trip to Abilene, Texas, from Coleman, Texas, on a hot, humid day in a car with a broken air conditioner. Once the suggestion is made that they go to Abilene, they all agree and pile in. When they return,

---

[100] *The Abilene Paradox*, (Carlsbad, CA: CRM, 2002).

someone says, "That was a great trip, wasn't it?" Finally someone says no, and they all open up and talk about how they never wanted to go in the first place—even the person who made the suggestion!

Harvey refers to this as the inability to manage agreement. It is people striving to get along so much that they will not speak out when they disagree. He says that this is caused by things such as action anxiety, imagined risk, peer pressure, and the fear of being thought of as naïve.

Action anxiety is simply being afraid to do or say something. Imagined risk is just fantasizing that something really bad may result. For example, people may be afraid to talk to the boss because they think the boss might get upset; when in reality the boss might want to hear from them. To make this point, the video depicts a couple planning a wedding; neither of the two wants to go through with it, but each is afraid to say anything out of fear that the other's mother might drop dead at the news. Peer pressure is a fear to rock the boat because others won't like you. And lastly, no one wants to be thought of as naïve.

The Abilene Paradox may be very important in the initial stages of group development as defined in *Managing for Excellence*. In the membership phase, members will strive for agreement and can go places they don't want to for conformity and maintaining pleasant social interactions. The paradox is similar to the issues of groupthink, in which a group strives to obtain agreement.

Groupthink is a phenomenon in which the groups' desire for harmony overrides realistic concerns about the alternatives. Most of the research on this is attributed to Irving Janis, a research psychologist from Yale University. A long list of events is thought to have been influenced by groupthink, including the Challenger Space Shuttle disaster, Pearl Harbor, the Bay of Pigs Invasion, and many more. In groupthink the decision makers engage in actions that tend to limit the introduction and evaluation of concerns that are contrary to the desired outcome of the group. Chaleff says that "cohesiveness can become a weakness ... and a need, regardless of the cost, for unanimity."[101] In the end, "groupthink screens out data and views that challenge."[102]

The elements of groupthink include things such as mind guards, isolation of the group, closed-mindedness, rationalization, stereotyping, illusions of invulnerability, illusions of anonymity, direct pressure, unquestioned belief in the morality of the group, and self-censorship. CRM produced a good training video to demonstrate a theory of how groupthink played a part in the Challenger Space Shuttle disaster. Other accounts claim some elements of groupthink were missing, and therefore, it was not a factor. The training video is very good, and taken along with the accounts from the Senate hearings on the disaster, I believe groupthink was a plausible factor.

The Challenger disaster video shows an engineer adamantly protesting the launch, warning that the O-rings have not been tested at the low temperatures they will be experiencing at launch time. He cites factual blow-by data and suggests the rings may not seal in the colder temperatures. The resulting discussions are fairly accurately portrayed between Morton-Thiokol (the company that manufactured the booster rockets) and NASA in an effort to reach consensus on whether or not to launch under the extreme cold conditions.

I learned that the pilots of the shuttle were aware of these concerns. I did not think that a space shuttle pilot would be concerned with such an issue, but all pilots are required to understand all performance, handling, and limitations of their aircraft. They asked if the issue of the O-rings had been resolved prior to launch and were told it was safe. We all know the decision was to launch—and the results were disastrous.

Groupthink involves mind guards and closed-minded thinking, or the "Don't try to confuse me with facts, I've made up my mind" approach. It involves rationalization: "It has worked before—why not again?" It may involve stereotyping as weak or stupid those individuals who are not on board with the group. Invulnerability is the idea that the groups' product

---

[101] Chaleff, *The Courageous Follower*, 92.
[102] Ibid., 93.

has been proven safe on prior occasions, thus it will prove to be safe in the future. The idea of anonymity is essentially, "The company guarantees this—not me." Direct pressure presents this question: "Do you want to be responsible for the change, the product not going into production, or the failure of the mission?" In self-censorship, a person just gives up and chooses to quit fighting. The belief in the morality of the group asks and assumes, "We all want what is best for the group, don't we?"

All of this is done in an effort to overcome resistance or disagreement, and come to agreement rather than exploring all the options and concerns with an open mind in order to come to the best possible choice. (Remember, we make choices not decisions, which is a big factor in avoiding groupthink.)

You can see issues of groupthink in our "Zen and the Art of Management" discussion in which we talked about not manipulating the group and the use of ambiguity as a leadership tool. After the Bay of Pigs incident, President Kennedy purposely avoided some meetings on the Cuban Missile Crisis in order to avoid influencing the group toward a specific outcome. Can you see how the Pygmalion Effect may have a part in groupthink? Can you see how paradigms may play a part in groupthink?

What are the ways we avoid groupthink? Clearly a practice of encouraging dissent is necessary to prevent groupthink. You can see how important it is not to allow cynics to be involved in the membership of the group, as they are good at creating the elements that contribute to groupthink. Promoting courage and a safe environment in which to speak are essential to avoiding groupthink.

Keeping the group focused on the goals/vision and remembering principle versus preference will also aid in minimizing groupthink. Most groupthink articles claim it is necessary to assign each person the role of critical evaluator. I would hope we would always do that, but it does not work if you have not created an expectation of approachability.

It is also suggested that the group use outside experts and consultants; I would agree but also suggest that you trust the expert opinions and verify factual data. A lot of the process in groupthink becomes emotional rather than factual. The group members begin to use emotional arguments to try to force others to ignore the facts and go along with the group.

It is not necessary that the group members agree totally on the choices that the group makes. The group will need to come to a consensus about a course of action. A consensus is not total agreement; "a consensus means getting no objections or the absence of undermining and interference in any given activity. It does not mean that everyone has the same opinion, idea or strategy. It does mean that all participating members have a say."[103] It is not a simple majority vote.

Cunningham and I were looking for some way to explore this in class, and we chose to take a look at an old Western movie, *The Oxbow Incident*[104], starring Henry Fonda. We developed an exercise to accompany the film, as it is a great vehicle to examine group dynamics, dysfunctional group behavior, and the ways that leaders can control a group.

In the movie, a respected cattle rancher is rumored to have been murdered by cattle rustlers. The local townspeople are very disturbed and form a posse, which is really nothing more than a lynch mob. The mob rushes out, under the direction of a retired army officer, and catches three suspects. The mob spends some time debating the issue, with a few people dissenting. They vote, and by majority rule, they hang the three suspects without a trial. The sheriff catches up to the mob, informs them that the rancher did not die and that the real culprits are in custody. He discovers the lynching, and everyone heads back to town. Henry Fonda's character gives a good speech at the end about the importance of justice, laws, and due process.

In class we discuss how the group was influenced by the emotions that overcame the course of action everyone knew to be right. The people were doing something they knew was wrong, but they willingly jumped on the bandwagon to get it done. We discuss how to regain control once a group is headed down that path. These conversations allow us to explore mob

---

103 Bennis and Nanus, *Leaders*, (New York: Harper and Row, 1985), 120.
104 *The Oxbow Incident*, Twentieth Century Fox, 1943

mentality, dysfunctional groups, majority rule, democracy, and justice, all in an effort to help us understand the different perspectives leaders must deal with when handling group dynamics. One of my favorite explorations is this: "Do the rules exist to protect the organization, the community, or a weak and powerless leader?" What do you think?

People tend to follow people of shared values. Just like in the selection process in chapter 1, we tend to choose to be with people we like. A leader can lead the group astray using many of the things we have discussed. For example, Hitler was a leader who used emotion, but was an evil person. Emotion is the key in creating a dysfunctional group but is also necessary in legitimately communicating vision. The leadership example I am hoping to convey is one of principle-based leadership qualities.

Evil leadership distorts the principles through the use of emotion. Such a leader might say something like, "We must eliminate those people because their very existence will take the food out of your child's mouth," or "Justice is too slow, so we must take it into our own hands to protect our families." Dysfunctional leaders build on emotion, blaming others for misfortune and breaking down the social rules that maintain order.

As a leader, you need to establish the facts to override the emotion. Strong emotions can trample values and principles; it takes a strong leader to bring people back to reality. During those times you may need to make a withdrawal from the account of trust that you have built up through trust, kindness, courtesy, and earning the respect of your followers.

People are leaders because others allow them to lead and follow them willingly. This amounts to people allowing you to have power over them; they are giving you permission to lead. Once you build up that trust, power, and respect, you may be able to make a withdrawal from that account in instances such as this. It is the only way that saying, "Trust me, that is a bad thing to do," is going to work. In *The 7 Habits*, Dr. Covey calls this an emotional bank account.[105]

---

[105] Covey, Stephen R., *The 7 Habits of Highly Effective People*, 188–90.

If you do not have that relationship with the group, you may need to add more than facts. Some courage (combined with a reminder of what is legal and the penalty for violating the law) might help. It may start to look like the Wild West, with the sheriff standing in front of the jail confronted by the lynch mob and saying, "You have to come through me to get to him." The dysfunctional leader at the front of the mob says, "There's only one of you and lots of us—you can't stop us all." The sheriff will reply, "Yep, but I'll get you, and you, and you, and you, and maybe two more of you before you get me, so who's first?"

During the stages of group development, a leader will need to watch for signs of groupthink and dysfunction. Those are times that the leader may need to intervene if the group is unable to sort it out for themselves. As the group moves through the stages, there will be opportunities for groupthink to develop. Even after the group moves into the shared responsibility stage, the possibility for groupthink is still present. A leader will need to watch carefully as the group moves through the stages and intervene if necessary to overcome a dysfunctional group dynamic.

Bradford and Cohen describe the stages of group development in *Managing for Excellence* [106] (mentioned briefly in chapter 3). The first is membership; as the group is coming together they try to be cautious and decide how much of themselves to invest into the group. The stage is already set for self-censorship and groupthink. The second stage is subgrouping, during which members struggle to find a place to belong. There is little chance that someone will say things in this stage that upset the group, and there is a very good likelihood of a trip to Abilene. The third stage is confrontation; after finding support from others, some individuals attempt to take a controlling position. This can be where stereotyping and direct pressure begin to show. The fourth stage is individual differentiation, during which the members are confident enough to shed subgroup ties and stand alone on their individual merits or expertise. The problem is that the members may only be interested in completing the individual assignments and are

---

[106] Bradford and Cohen, *Managing for Excellence*, 188–203. Obert, S. L. "The Development of Organizational Task Groups" (PhD Dissertation) (Cleveland, Case-Western Reserve University, 1979).

not really looking to problem solve for the group, so isolation and closed-mindedness are very real elements of groupthink in this stage.

Finally the last stage, shared responsibility, is one which Bradford and Cohen believe many groups never get to. In this area the team is moving forward with the overarching goal, vision, and mission in mind. They are committed to excellence and helping each other reach the goals by holding each other accountable and providing assistance when necessary. In this stage there is a definite possibility of the illusions of invulnerability, anonymity, and the inherent morality of the group taking hold.

This area is difficult to reach and requires a skillful leader. The leader will need to have all the qualities, values, and traits we have discussed to keep the team members focused and motivated. This is where the science and the art must come together; it is where these traits and values held deeply by the leader are recognizable and clearly communicated to the members. It is where the members become loyal, willing, and courageous followers—not of the leader, but of the shared values and vision.

Fill the Holes

In the early years of the program, we used *Kent State*[107] by James Michener (along with Dr. Covey's *7 Habits)* during this portion of the course to give us a look at leaders and groups. I thought *Kent State* was a magnificent book, as Michener showed the values of the characters and how they all played parts in the eventual shooting of four people on the college campus in May of 1970. Most people know about the shooting but really have little understanding of the events that led up to that fateful day.

The book goes into the emotional influence that subversive groups such as the Weathermen and Students for a Democratic Society (SDS) had on the campus groups and students. It describes the inaction and leadership failures of the campus administration, the city government, the campus police, the city police, civic groups, the FBI, and the National Guard. It

---

107 Michener, James A., *Kent State: What Happened and Why* (New York: Random House and Reader's Digest Association, 1971).

provides an opportunity to review how groupthink and other group dynamics played a part in a hugely dysfunctional event.

The National Guard had been pulled from a truckers' strike to respond to the campus of Kent State. The Guard had been on duty for several days without rest and, like most National Guard units, was made up of just regular citizens with limited training. They were a military unit that was thrust into a civilian situation where they had to deal with students and a school town mentality that was different from what they had been trained for.

The Guard arrived at Kent State on Saturday night to restore order during the burning of the ROTC building. On Sunday night the Guard dealt with a riot in the town of Kent. Using fixed bayonets, members of the Guard stabbed at least two (and maybe as many as seven) students during the riot. On Monday, the day of the shooting, the closest person shot was seventy-one feet from the Guard's skirmish line; the farthest was 745 feet away. Fifty-five rounds were fired by the Guard into the crowd; thirteen people were hit, and four were killed (some believe that one other person was hit, but this was never officially reported).

I mention this because history tends to repeat itself. The Occupy Wall Street movement of late is another example of a group backed by subversive elements (anarchists and anticonsumer groups) and civilian leadership that failed to properly evaluate and then take appropriate action. Amazingly, there was large public support for the Occupy protesters, who themselves had little or no idea what the movement was really about. Emotion and dysfunctional group dynamics were at the heart of this situation again.

In the early years of the leadership program, the instructors were a work in progress and in various stages of group development. We tried to maintain that stage of shared responsibility. Working on the program for the seventh session was a great example of that effort.

In order to further explore group concepts, our instructors reviewed a book for the seventh session that would thrust our groups into some turmoil and help us examine how far we had grown as a class. We debated using the book because we felt that the police officers in the program might reject it.

For one of our biannual instructor meetings, Cunningham brought in *A Taste of Power* by Elaine Brown,[108] a book we eventually adopted for the seventh session. Elaine Brown was the head of the Black Panther Party (BPP) for a period of time. Brown says that she took control of the party while Huey Newton was in self-exile in Cuba; I liked to say that she was in charge when Huey fled the United States to avoid prosecution for murder (I suppose either explanation has truth to it depending upon your paradigm). Cunningham thought it would be a good book for this session, as it would stretch the group's understandings and paradigms. We all reviewed the book and came back to the next meeting with some opinions.

Brown continually referred to police officers as pigs and supported killing them; by contrast, she referred to the Panthers as heroes and freedom fighters. Some of us thought this might not go over well with our audience. We argued over this all day during our meeting, continuing into the night over dinner and all the next day. Another of the instructors brought *The Shadow of the Panther* by Hugh Pearson to look at in place of Brown's book.[109] The group chose to look at that one also, as Cunningham chose to experiment with Brown's book in a class.

Pearson's book was very factual and not nearly as inflammatory as Brown's. In fact, he did not have nice things to say about Brown, but he did give a great perspective on the development of the black power movement in America. I found Pearson's book very informative and fascinating, and it opened up ideas, perspectives, and paradigms I had not thought of. As a result, it gave me a new perspective on Brown's paradigm and book, also showing me how we could learn from it. I now saw it as a new aha experience on leadership.

---

[108] Brown, Elaine, *A Taste of Power* (New York: Pantheon Books, 1992).
[109] Pearson, Hugh, *The Shadow of the Panther* (Reading, MA: Addison-Wesley Publishing, 1994).

I came to see Brown's book as just what we wanted for the seventh session. While group members were reading the book, emotion would surface, and keeping that factual edge to focus on the vision could slip away. It was a great opportunity to just let the book work and then try to bring the group back to reality. Sometimes that was a difficult task, because it was not easy to overcome such ingrained hatred on both sides of this book, or the racial issues.

We have already discussed how important it is for the leader to keep an open mind and solicit all ideas and information to make informed choices. Discussion of this book presented an opportunity to really study and test the groupthink dynamics, the idea of closed-mindedness, mind guards, and so on, and use them in an experiential learning situation.

We also used a short video from the documentary miniseries *Eyes on the Prize*[110] that showed interviews with Elaine Brown and others in the Black Panther Party. I found one segment of particular interest; it showed Fred Hampton, a BPP member, conducting a meeting. Brown described him as very charismatic and not a racist. I'm not sure we can agree on that, but that is not the point I'm interested in discussing here.

An interesting point for leadership is that the BPP came into power and got a lot of support from many areas you would not have expected. Pearson explained why that was possible. Black Americans had historically been treated to a lack of justice and fairness. They were embittered people with opportunities taken away at every turn (something akin to grounds for mutiny). As the peaceful protests of the sixties failed with the murder of Martin Luther King Jr., this left an opening for the BPP to fill in for many who felt it was time to refuse to be pushed around anymore. This is an important lesson for leaders; when there is a lack of leadership, someone will fill the void.

In this case, the void was filled by the BPP and Huey Newton. Regardless of the lawlessness of the party and the fact that they supported the overthrow

---

[110] *Eyes on the Prize 2*, "A Nation of Law, 1968–1971 (Episode 6)", PBS, 1990.

of the government, they began to run programs and provide help to the people. They began a breakfast program for the underprivileged children who could not afford breakfast for school. The government attacked these programs, further empowering the Panthers. The government attacked a BPP headquarters and burned the food supplies in the process. Regardless of the justification, the community was upset by the action.

There were organized attacks on BPP houses and headquarters, falsified reports, and unfair arrests and sentencing, which only empowered the Panthers even more. The head of the FBI, J. Edgar Hoover, called the Panthers the greatest threat to American society. Instead of taking the opportunity for leadership, the government and law enforcement acted in ways that caused the community to perceive them as fighting against the people they should have helped. If Fred Hampton had been the charismatic leader he appeared to be, maybe the government could have worked with him. The government could have been empowered by working with him, supporting the breakfast program and other initiatives to support the children and educational needs of the community. If the Panthers had refused to partner with the government and the government had still provided aid, it could have taken power from the Panthers.

As leaders, we should be looking for opportunities to lead. It is how companies such as Zappos, Amazon, and Facebook get a foothold in the market. It is how Pepsi, Coca-Cola, Wal-Mart and so many others began; they seized opportunities. In the Kent State incident, the government should have taken the lead and avoided the situation. In the Occupy movement, the government and Wall Street missed a giant opportunity to deal with the needs of the people. I am not talking about the crazies who think the Rose Parade is a militarized operation of an oppressive government backed by the banking industry; I'm talking about the people who say they supported the movement. My advice to the government would be, "If they are protesting, come to their aid, take the responsibility and power from them, and lead; they are offering an opportunity and are too stupid to realize it. Seize the opportunity for leadership and fill the holes." I am in no way suggesting tolerance of illegal acts or civil disobedience though. Action to maintain order is the duty of government.

In class we used a complex staff meeting exercise to examine group dynamics. The exercise had a number of components that were tempting in the wrong hands. These elements could cause the entire project to go sideways if not controlled to some degree by the student leaders of the exercise. The learning goal was to have the students attempt to avoid groupthink, but totally fall into groupthink by the afternoon without realizing it.

In the exercise, students met and made a plan for an imaginary organization to improve stated performance goals while dealing with some significant personnel issues. The plan was presented to the CEO, boss, or commander at the end of the morning session. The boss rejected it and made some pretty significant demands for change. The students were upset with the requested changes. We then provided them with several options to pursue; they could talk with the boss to change or modify their plan, ask for explanations, or just implement the changes with their sections. In the afternoon, we included role playing and video recording for all options.

The amazing part is that they get so caught up in fighting for their preferences that they fail to see how the principles and the actions demanded by the boss are very similar to their own ideas. Groupthink sets in full force. It is not until near the end of the exercise, when the facilitators begin to focus the group on the big picture, that the group members realize they have made a mistake. The boss is completely right with one exception; the boss failed to communicate the vision and obtain the necessary support and buy-in. This leads us into a discussion of the leader's job in organizational change. The status quo is acceptable to managers; *leaders take chances and create change.*

Change

I believe change has three phases: first, recognizing we need a change; second, choosing an option; and third, phasing in the option. William Bridges has a book on managing transitions and offers training/management consulting in that area. He proposes that the three stages in organizational transitions are endings, the neutral zone, and new beginnings.[111] He provides a simple explanation of the stages of change that is easy to interpret.

---

[111] Bridges, William, *Managing Transitions: Making the Most of Change* (Boston: Da Capo Press, 2009).

The endings stage is where people need to let go of the old way of doing things. These include such things as defending your turf or areas you might consider your own personal little section or job. This includes familiar or comfortable procedures and possibly personal relationships or friendships as well. People develop self-esteem and pride in knowing their jobs and appearing competent in their work.

The next phase can be described as the time between the old process and the new process, and it involves fear and anxiety about the new process. Bridges refers to this as the neutral zone or valley of despair since anxiety, overload, and morale problems can be expected. I think this starts as soon as there is an announcement about the impending change.

The next stage—implementing the change—is the one Bridges calls the beginnings area or new equilibrium. In any change new skills must be acquired, and there is a need to restore confidence and form new relationships. Bridges explains that the manager's job is to prepare for the transitions, explain, show/demonstrate, observe, and supervise. What do you think the leader's job is?

In *Flight of the Buffalo*,[112] James Belasco and Ralph Stayer discuss the importance of allowing employees to lead, reflecting the bottom-up leadership principles we have been discussing throughout this book. Employees need to have ownership in the process; they must be empowered as a part of the vision.

Leaders get the team involved in the process from the beginning. Chances are good that the people who are doing the work can see more efficient ways of accomplishing it. They probably have a better understanding of the hands-on procedures than management does. We do not want to implement systems and procedures that make the process more difficult. If there are management factors that need to be considered in the changes, explain them to the team. The members should be treated like adults; they are capable of understanding management's needs.

---

112 Belasco, James A. and Stayer, Ralph C., *Flight of the Buffalo*, (New York: Warner Books, 1993).

It goes back to all the leadership traits we have been discussing: power and empowerment; accountability and responsibility; pride, professionalism, and productivity; the Pygmalion Effect, and so on. We do not lead with a "my way or the highway" attitude.

When we look at change, we need to consider a number of factors:

- What are the cost/profit factors?
- What is the social climate?
- What is the resistance?
- What support do we have? Is there a need?
- Does the technology exist to support it?
- Is the timing right?
- What equipment do we need?
- What personnel do we need?
- Is there training available?
- Is there time to build the training programs?
- Will it work?
- Do we have time to prepare?
- How do we present the change?
- How do we manage the change?
- Are there options?
- How can we evaluate this?
- Do we have trust, respect, and a past record of success?
- What is the history?

This is only a partial list. How many more can you add?

There are so many issues for a leader to consider regarding change. It is essential that the change is communicated to all the people who may be affected by it. This cannot be done by a memo (think back to the example of the new motto given to the police department); it must be done by personal interaction, with assurances that it will not threaten the security of the people involved. The leader needs to sell the changes to the whole organization, not just to management. It is a part of sharing the vision, overarching goals, and values. This may require a withdrawal from the emotional bank account, so be sure you have deposited funds in that account.

Change is likely to be more successful in an organization in which creativity and individuals are valued. Change will be more acceptable if employees are involved from the onset in evaluating the need for change and in creating, designing, and implementing the change, and if they will share in or benefit from the change.

Leaders communicate vision, values, and the need for change. All of the factors we discussed in our conversations about "Zen and the Art of Management" come into play when we look at change. Leaders are change agents. Leaders manage risk and motivate people to follow, always operating in a developer mode and always moving forward to a future vision of the organization.

We looked at Billy Mitchell in this segment of the program as a case study in change. Today Billy Mitchell is largely considered to be the father of the US Air Force, but this was not the case in his own time. After WWI, Billy Mitchell was a general in the Army Air Corp. There was not a real vision for the Air Force, except through Mitchell's eyes. Most of the military leaders and government leaders saw airplanes as carnival entertainment and not serious weapons of war. There was little or no government development of aircraft at that time; most of it was being done in the private sector and in other countries.

When Mitchell returned to the United States, after the war, he became director of aviation resources under the secretary of the Air Service, stationed at Langley Field in Virginia. He directed most of the actual flying activities at the time. Because there was a shortage of funds after the war, Congress wanted to downsize funding for both the Army and the Navy. In 1921, there were several demonstrations to evaluate aircraft as weapons under wartime conditions. The demonstrations were staged to evaluate air attacks on naval vessels as compared to ship-to-ship combat. Both would have an opportunity to sink large war ships captured and decommissioned after the war.

Mitchell had been campaigning endlessly for the Air Service and had a vision of the effectiveness of aircraft for combat in the future. Unfortunately, Mitchell was restricted to existing wartime conditions for his demonstrations and therefore had to restrict the size of the bombs and the altitude for attacks.

Mitchell knew that the conditions favored the Navy, and he begged General "Black Jack" Pershing for a waiver to carry larger bombs. He was denied the waiver, but did it anyway, successfully sinking the ships. The military was upset with Mitchell. Eventually he was demoted to colonel and transferred to Fort Sam Houston, Texas, where he served in a non-flying position. After some time and several incidents that resulted in the deaths of many aviators under his former command, Mitchell chose to make a public statement in which he called the military command "treasonous." His purpose was to draw attention to his cause, but of course, that did not go over well. He was arrested and court-martialed. After his trial, conviction, and suspension from duty, Mitchell resigned from the service and died of a number of ailments in 1936.

The movie *The Court-Martial of Billy Mitchell*[113] is adequate to review Mitchell's career for the purpose of discussing change. During Mitchell's career, he envisioned all the things that the Japanese used against us in Pearl Harbor as well as the future of jet aircraft, bombers, and so on. In 1942 President Franklin Roosevelt posthumously elevated Mitchell to the rank of major general and nominated him for the Congressional Gold Medal, eventually awarded in 1946, for his extraordinary vision of the future of air power.

Mitchell was such a visionary, but he was like Jonathan, the reckless young bird in the book *Jonathan Livingston Seagull*, who alienated the command staff (flock) to the point that they banished him. Mitchell tried hard to move the Air Service forward to becoming the US Air Force, but he may have actually delayed the development.

---

113 *The Court-Martial of Billy Mitchell*, United States Pictures, 1955.

Sometimes you have a great idea, but you are not the person to bring it about, or it may not be the appropriate time to present it. If the idea is good and you are that unselfish leader, then choosing to have it presented by another person who may be more effective is a necessary element in being a good leader. Leadership is not about you; it is about moving the group toward success.

Mitchell failed to use many of the elements for change. The technology did not exist at the time, nor did the money. There was lots of resistance, and he did not look for support. He was definitely not the guy to push the program, and there were options in the private sector to pursue. In class I drew a picture of a brick wall on a chart and asked everyone what happens if you just keep running your head into a wall? I always remember the first thing my self-defense instructor taught me in the police academy, "If what you are doing is not working, try something else!"

We always play win/win. This means we work for the mutual benefit of all parties involved. If people want to play win/lose, then we choose not to play. We always begin with a vision of the future or with *the end in mind* (as Dr. Covey says in his Habit 2). Leaders are always looking at the long term, keeping the big perspective in focus, and focusing on the whole *and* the parts.

Spencer Johnson wrote *Who Moved My Cheese?*,[114] a short, fun book about change and how to manage it. Not only does this book help with organizational change, but it will help you as the leader manage change in your life, because as Johnson says, "change happens, they keep moving the cheese!" This book will help you deal with changes in any number of areas, from the price of coffee at Starbucks to a major incident such as a divorce or job loss. Everything we deal with in a business setting has direct application to everything we deal with in our personal lives. Johnson must have been in my self-defense class, because he says the same things that the instructor drilled into us.

---

[114] Johnson, Spencer, MD, *Who Moved My Cheese?* (New York: G.P. Putnam's Sons, 1998).

Johnson warns that we must anticipate change. Get ready for the cheese to move. Monitor change. Smell the cheese often. Anticipate what needs to change. Look for the opportunities (such as the BPP's opportunity to rise to power). Adapt to the change quickly, as the quicker you let go of the old cheese, the quicker you can enjoy the new cheese (Bridge's stage two, valley of despair). Take action, and be proactive (not reactive, back to Covey and Frankl). Enjoy the change. Savor the taste of new cheese, but be ready for change because someone will move your cheese again—they always do!

Review and Evaluation

Look for situations that may involve groupthink issues. See how many trips to Abilene you can avoid with your family and friends. In your next meeting look at how much control there is and think about whether it stifles creativity or tends to create elements of groupthink.

How often do you demand dissent from your team members? Are they afraid to give opinions? What can you do to encourage them to provide appropriate feedback? How often does the boss demand dissent? How often is the boss provided with dissent? Are you afraid to provide appropriate feedback, and is this fear based on something real? What kind of obedience is expected in your organization or by you? Do you expect blind obedience, and what effects will that have on your leadership traits?

Think about what kinds of changes can happen to you, and consider how you can best prepare to seize the opportunities they present.

Notes

Chapter Seven

Learning to Lead in the Spiderweb

Teaching to Learn Respect

A friend's daughter told me she was totally frustrated with having to write a paper based on the book *Zen and the Art of Motorcycle Maintenance* for a college philosophy class. She said the paper had to be at least three pages and she did not know were to start. I told her, "I feel your pain, and I think I can help." As I started thinking about how to help her, I remembered when I went through the leadership program as a student in a pilot class. I was singled out by Lieutenant Cunningham to lead a discussion on day one of the seventh session.

He asked me to lead a discussion on success, respect, and discipline as a review on areas we had already covered. I was terrified but figured I had some time to prepare, so I asked when the discussion would be. He said, "We are taking a five-minute break, and then you got it!" "Wow," I said, "I don't know where to start." Cunningham told me to just think about the difference between courage and confidence, about Frankl, and about quality; then he walked away.

So I sat, diligently scouring my notes and books and racking my brain for a way to proceed without looking like a complete fool. I had been stupid enough to invite my chief of police (who had been appointed by the governor to sit on the Peace Officer Standards and Training Commission for the state) to attend that day of class. He was seated with the class and had no idea of what was about to happen. I felt like Charlie Brown; I was going to miss the ball and be the heel. Or worse, the Wallenda factor might take hold, and I'd fall off the high wire.

Class resumed, and I started off by asking, "What is success?" The group immediately bit into the concept with a vibrant discussion, and off we went. I looked like a genius. But the discussion was successful for one reason; the group stepped up to help me. All the time I was up there, ideas were rattling through my head about different ways to direct the dialogue to cover topics and related concepts. After about an hour, Cunningham suggested we all take a break. I was exhausted. My brain had turned to mush, but I was so excited about what had happened. I could not believe how much I had just learned.

On the break, my classmates congratulated me, and my chief complimented me. Meanwhile, my brain was still trying to process what had occurred. As I went on to teach with Cunningham in future classes, he challenged me again and again to step up and be a leader with new challenges and new material.

I believe you get a third of the information by being a student, another third by teaching and sharing, and the last third through a never-ending process of research, thought and discovery. I learned amazing things in each class just by listening to others and examining my own paradigm with the new information and thoughts.

In each class I facilitated, I did something similar to what Cunningham had done with me. I would pick out several people to lead the discussions and the direction of the class in the seventh session (though I gave them a little more heads-up and discussion time before tossing them into the group). This all varied depending on the different classes and personalities, but the concept of exploration remained the same.

I would start off by briefing them with a discussion on the concepts of success, respect, discipline, courage, and confidence. They knew the concepts and the principles and only needed to rely on Self 2 to lead the discussions. I reminded them that courage was acting on values. Confidence is what we get when we do something over and over—success through repetition. It can certainly be based on similar elements as courage, but where we get into trouble is with overconfidence. If the confidence is not based on values but on simple repetition, we may be challenged in defending our positions. When we lead from positions based on courage and values, it is difficult to trip us, confuse us, and derail us as we carry out our missions. When we operate this way, there is nothing to try to remember or repeat; instead we lead through ingrained values and principles.

Frankl defined success as something that ensues, just as Pirsig tried to capture quality in *Zen and the Art of Motorcycle Maintenance*; it is an elusive thing that ensues as the result of caring and a combination of art and science. Pirsig tried to define the parameters of quality but ended up going crazy chasing the concept. You can do the same with success.

If an employee works in the mailroom all his life and always does a mediocre or poor job, does that make him successful? If that poorly performing employee raises a family and puts the kids through college, is he a success in the eyes of the family? Is success something that is merely in the eye of the beholder, or is there some quantifiable definition of success?

If I defined success as the accomplishment of goals within societal guidelines, ethics and personal values that are uniform to the principles, would you agree? Do you think success is being loved and admired by others? Is success obtaining wealth? Is success having your child tell others how much they love you as a father or mother? I would hope by now that you would want to explore this a little more with yourself and others before you summarize and bring closure. This is nothing more than an opportunity to explore and learn through dialogue.

We also want to review discipline. I think all discipline is self-discipline and all motivation is self-motivation. In chapter 1 we learned Drucker's thoughts that development was not the responsibility of the organization, but the responsibility of the individual, so this would be a logical path to explore. There are ways to attempt to motivate people or to demoralize people; in the end, though, it is always their choice to get motivated or not. Remember, we are looking at leadership, so we need to keep this in mind as we explore.

Every book referenced in this study of leadership makes clear that working on yourself is essential. This is why *The Sea Wolf*,[115] the last book used in the program, is such an interesting study. *The Sea Wolf* is a Jack London novel that provides a great perspective on the battle between good and evil, respect and fear.

In *The Sea Wolf*, Humphrey Van Weyden falls overboard from a ferry boat in San Francisco Bay and is saved by the crew of the *Ghost*, Wolf Larson's seal-hunting schooner. "Hump," as he is called, is taken in as part of the crew as Captain Wolf Larson forges on with no thought of returning him to San Francisco. It begins a journey for Hump to explore his values and find himself. Wolf takes a liking to him and enjoys conversations with him, since both he and Hump are well-studied intellectuals.

However, Wolf is of the belief that it is every man for himself and only the strong deserve to survive. Hump fears Wolf for his strength and brutality on board the ship, but also learns to respect him for his knowledge and abilities. During the voyage, Wolf goes on to challenge Hump's values, discipline, and knowledge in a game of cat and mouse. Hump learns to understand and discipline himself, but he also lives in constant fear of Wolf.

Hump feared Wolf, as did most everyone on board the *Ghost*. Possibly that could have equated to respect for Wolf, but they are not the same. I may say that I have a fear of the ocean. I am not afraid to go out in the water. I know that it can hurt me if I get in over my head; so, perhaps it is a healthy respect for the ocean. Flying is very similar; you must never lose respect for the aircraft or all the physics involved. Flying can kill you in a flash, but I do not have a fear of flying. Respect is something we want as leaders, but is fear an element of respect?

---

[115] London, Jack, *The Sea Wolf*, first published in 1904, (Pleasantville, NY: Readers Digest, 1989).

As we explore respect, I like to start from about 1490 AD to 1520 AD with Machiavelli and *The Prince*. Machiavelli asks the question, "Is it better to be loved or feared?" He answered that it is better to have both, but men love at their own will and fear at the will of the prince. This excerpt from *The Prince* is really interesting in helping us look at respect.

In chapter 17 of *The Prince*[116] ("Of Cruelty and Clemency and Whether it is Better to be Loved or Feared"), Niccolo Machiavelli writes:

Proceeding to the other qualities before named, I say that every prince must desire to be considered merciful and not cruel. He must, however, take care not to misuse this mercifulness. ...

The prince, therefore, must not mind incurring the charge of cruelty for the purpose of keeping his subjects united and faithful, for, with a very few examples, he will be more merciful than those who, from excess tenderness, allow disorders to arise from which spring bloodshed and rapine for these as a rule injure the whole community, while the executions carried out by the prince injure only the individuals...

From this arises the question whether it is better to be loved more than feared. The reply is that one ought to be both feared and loved, but it is difficult for the two to go together. It is much safer to be feared than loved if one of the two has to be wanting. For it may be said of men in general that they are ungrateful, voluble, dissemblers, anxious to avoid danger and covetous of gain, as long as you benefit them, they are entirely yours, they offer their blood, their goods, their life and their children, as I have before said, when the necessity is remote, but when it approaches they revolt. And the prince who has relied solely on their words without making other preparations is ruined, for friendship which is gained by purchase and not secured through grandeur and nobility of spirit is bought but not secured and in a pinch is not to be expended in your service. ...

---

[116] Machiavelli, Niccolo, *The Prince*, 1532, translation by Luigi Ricci, 1903 (New York: Oxford University Press, 1921). Reprinted with permission.

Lloyd J. Edwards Jr.

> I conclude therefore with regard to be loved or feared that men love at their own free will, but fear at the will of the prince, and that a wise prince must rely on what is in his power and not on what is in the power of others, and he must only avoid incurring hatred, as has been explained.

Most people think Machiavelli was brutal, ruthless, vicious, and evil. While *The Prince* has some definite differentiation between politics and ethics, it is not a work that purports evil. *The Prince* was written to explain how a monarch, more specifically, the ruler of Florence, should rule. In *The Prince*, Machiavelli expresses his belief in free will and self-determination, a new concept for the period. In his later work, *Discourses,* Machiavelli is very republican in nature, touting patriotism, virtues, and open political participation. So, we need to take a look at what he is saying in this brief excerpt.

At the beginning, Machiavelli is discussing the need for discipline and the need for the leader to enforce the rules fairly and appropriately to avoid disorder and chaos and to maintain the safety of the kingdom. He talks about not being afraid to incur a charge of cruelty because you enforce the rules and maintain order. He is referring to what we discussed in chapter 4 about principle versus preference, and in chapter 3, about establishing your values clearly to the organization.

We can relate this to very personal issues of raising children; it is necessary sometimes to punish them to be sure they understand certain issues. This is for their safety and so that they don't repeat problematic behaviors. We use the same methods in our working relationships. So, does that make punishment and the use of fear motivation? Is that the way we want to lead? Is fear a necessary and initial step in establishing discipline? Is the establishment of rules, limitations, and consequences something you have control over? Is Machiavelli correct in stating that the use of fear is safer?

We usually finish off our dialogue without any clear definitions of what success, discipline, and respect are. In fact, we may end up more confused than we thought we were when we started, but that is just fine. Remember the right question is far more important than the right answer. We find it necessary to keep exploring through dialogue in search of the truth. We do not want a conclusion; as Postman describes in *Teaching as a Subversive Activity,* the good teacher rarely summarizes or brings closure that ends further thought. I want you to learn to think about the concepts and how they fit into your paradigm. Now we just take a break to digest the thought, and shift gears to move into another related subject. So, are you ready to lead this discussion?

Don't Try to Bluff Me

We watched the movie *Patton*[117] in class, not just because it is a really great movie, but because we want to explore fear, bluff, and ego as they relate to leadership. If we go back to *Twelve O'Clock High* we see another example of fear, bluff, and ego presented by General Savage. Savage is a very caring, compassionate person who has a job to do, so to accomplish this he plays a role as a hard-tailed wing commander. He makes this very evident when he and his sergeant driver, Ernie, are driving to the 918th for the first time to assume command. They stop for a cigarette before entering the gate, and the two men step out of the front seat of the car. Savage asks Ernie if he would like a smoke. After a few moments, he changes his role and says, "Let's go, Sergeant"—no longer referring to his driver by his first name. Ernie quickly responds, snapping to attention and opening the back door for the general. Savage is now in his role as the leader.

In one section of *Patton*, in which George C. Scott plays the title character, the general is in headquarters planning an attack. He begins to rant, saying, "If we are not successful, let no one come back alive!" This commands the immediate attention of all present. His aide quietly comes over to him afterward and tells him that sometimes they cannot tell when he is acting and when he is not. Patton replies, "It's not important for them to know; it's only important for me to know."

Clearly there is some role playing going on with these leaders, but Patton also had some ego working as well. Is ego a necessary element of the leader?

---

[117] *Patton*, Twentieth Century Fox, 1970

We want the leader to have courage, confidence, respect, knowledge, experience, humility, and compassion, but does that naturally result in a certain amount of ego? If ego is self-centered, then we need to leave ego behind. If ego is an alternative to the reality, then we need to leave ego behind. If ego is self-confidence, then we need to think about having a little of it since we always want to go into situations with the intent of success.

In this idea of role playing, the leader may be tempted to use bluff. Savage used bluff to some degree in challenging the pilots to transfer out of the bomb group. He really never expected them to take him up on that, and it would have been a complete disaster for the group, the command, the war, and Savage had they not changed their minds.

Patton also used bluff in a confrontation with General Lucian Truscott over a desire to coordinate Truscott's attack group with a larger effort. Truscott does not want to go along with the mission timeline and expresses his concerns and doubts to Patton. Patton first tries to cash in on some debt, reminding Truscott he recommended him for his Distinguished Service Medal. When that does not convince Truscott, Patton warns him that he can have him relieved and replace him with someone who can complete the task. Truscott calls his bluff and tells the general that he can replace him anytime he wants to. Of course, Patton does not have the luxury of replacing Truscott, so he reverts to ordering him to comply.

We have discussed power and how easy it is to lose as a leader. When you bluff someone, or try to manipulate them and fail, they will suddenly see that you no longer care about them, and you will instantly lose power and respect. Then you will return to operating out of fear only. Now all you have left is the threat of insubordination, which is the final tool available to a weak and powerless leader. At this point, you can consider that your leadership efforts are finished, and while you may complete the task, you have lost respect as the leader. It is always best to just be yourself—but remember, you are the leader, not just another one of the guys, so act the part.

Remember that spiderweb-looking thing I mentioned in the beginning, where all the concepts of leadership were tied together in such a complex matrix that it would be impossible to take one concept out and manage to keep the matrix together? Perhaps obtaining respect is in the center of this complex matrix of leadership, so let's go back to trying to figure out respect.

Machiavelli said essentially, "You can't buy me love" (so did John and Paul). I agree with Machiavelli; this idea that everyone will follow you only if they like you is nonsense:

> And the prince who has relied solely on their words without making other preparations is ruined, for friendship which is gained by purchase and not secured through grandeur and nobility of spirit is bought but not secured and in a pinch is not to be expended in your service[118].

What the heck is "grandeur and nobility of spirit"? I get the part about friendship gained by purchase; this seems easy: To make you happy, I give you a couple of days off that you want, even though this hurts the team. The result is you will love me temporarily—that is until I need something from you that is inconvenient for you to give. Then you are going to love at your own will, not mine. This does not mean I do not try to accommodate your needs, but this is not leadership. In leadership people follow because they want to give the power to you to lead, not because they like you, but because they love you and respect you.

Do your kids love you? Do you love your parents? Do you love God and country? What is it that you care about more than yourself? What is the greater work that you must create, as Frankl described, to be successful?

Band of Brothers,[119] discussed earlier in this book, was a story about Easy Company, a combat unit in Europe during WWII. The unit leader, now Major Richard Winters, gave everything to keep the men of Easy Company together and safe. Everyone in Easy Company knew that Winters cared more about them than he did for himself, and they followed him without

---

118 Machiavelli, Niccolo, *The Prince*
119 *Band of Brothers*, HBO.

question. Everyone in Easy Company loved and respected Winters. Winters was truly a leader who possessed incredible courage balanced with humility and love.

Do your children know that you love them more than you love yourself? Do they do what you ask them to out of fear of punishment or fear of disappointment? Did Winters lead by grandeur and nobility of spirit? Does your family look to you to lead them with grandeur and nobility of spirit? How about your employees? In your description of the best leader, did that person have *grandeur and nobility of spirit*? Did he or she inspire you to *greatness, dignity, and a purity of the soul*? How about a pattern of *good works, integrity, reverence, incorruptibility, sound judgment and speech that cannot be condemned*? Are you trying to be that person?

Further defining grandeur and nobility of spirit might be as difficult as Pirsig's search to define quality or our attempts to define success. It certainly seems like we should all know what those things are, or at least recognize them when we see them. They are just so difficult to put into words. Maybe they exceed the science and the art sides of the equation to combine both, conceived through love and caring. I certainly wish I could tell you exactly how these things all work. I wish I could make them work for me all the time. If you have been playing along through this work, you probably know exactly what I mean, but may also find it difficult to explain. Maybe someday, someone will say you have it, and it will feel amazing. There is no greater reward for a leader than to know he or she has inspired others to excellence.

Please Forgive Me

No leader is going to be perfect. Everyone will make mistakes that disappoint or injure people in one way or another. In *The Prince*, Machiavelli is not an advocate of virtues (as we think of them) and compassion. He advocates that the ends justify the means if they are to the benefit of the prince and the state. His only warnings are to avoid hatred, punish fairly and swiftly, refrain from stealing land or capturing women, and try to honor your word. He even asserts that compassion and clemency are good so long as they benefit the prince. I do not believe the ends justify the means; I believe we lead through consistent, sound principles and values, one of which is forgiveness.

Forgiveness is a necessary element for leadership, and understanding it from different perspectives is essential. Admiral Stockdale, the commander of the American POWs in Vietnam, said, "It is neither American nor Christian to nag a repentant sinner to his grave."[120] In a quest for perfection we lose innovation and damage morale, risk taking, open thinking, and critical evaluation. It can, in and of itself, create groupthink. If we truly want to encourage and empower people, we must be prepared for some failures and consider them opportunities for learning and advancement, even if the failures are character related.

In police work, we talk about unforgivable sins such as lying, false reporting, stealing, and brutality. Those offenses are defined by law, and that makes it impossible to continue to employ as peace officers anyone who engages in those behaviors. We have talked about how a leader can influence the ethics of the organization and the individuals. We cannot forget that at some point we told a lie and someone forgave us for that. As a result, we learned a valuable lesson that reminded us of the damage that type of act causes and changed our behavior (back to Sundance and SEEs).

Excuses and blame do not work for leaders or followers. Dan Carlson wrote an article, "Hey, Who's Responsible for This Mess?" This provides some examples of what he refers to as "politicians' defense":

1. I didn't do it.
2. Okay, I did it, but it wasn't illegal.
3. Well, yes, it was illegal, but everyone else was doing it too, and besides, I was doing less of it.
4. Yes, I did it, but the means you used to catch me were inappropriate.
5. You are only picking on me because _____ (fill in the blank).[121]

---

[120] Manning, *The World of Epictetus*, 297.
[121] Carlson, Dan, *Hey, Who's Responsible for This Mess?*, Fall 1994 The Washington Post Writers Group, The Ethics Roll Call, 6–7.

According to research by sociologists Gresham Sykes and David Matza, juvenile delinquents justify (or neutralize) their behavior in five major ways. It does not take a great deal of imagination to recognize that all people sometimes use similar rationalizations to explain their own behavior:

1. Denial of responsibility: "It wasn't my fault." "Someone else caused this."
2. Denial of injury: "Nobody got hurt, so what's the problem?" "I know the policy prohibits ..., but it's only a minor error in the report."
3. Denial of the victim: "They deserved it." "They asked for it."
4. Condemnation of the condemners: "If you think what I did was bad, look at what he is doing." (Michael Josephson of the Josephson Institute for Ethics calls this the Theory of Relative Filth: "Yes, I'm dirty, but they are dirtier.")
5. Appeals to higher loyalties: "We have to stick together." "We are a family [or unit, team, gang, etc.]."[122]

Just simply admitting that you were wrong and asking forgiveness goes a long way with followers. Public figures know this, and there are books, references, and consulting firms that specialize in apologies. They will tell you what to say, what to admit, what not to say, how to say it, and even provide spokespersons to say it for you. If you want to remain a leader and protect the loss of respect and power, I really suggest you say it yourself. Make it simple, truthful, complete, and from the heart, which means you really must be sorry! People will forgive if you are forthcoming.

As for your followers, you need to be compassionate and understanding. If they are coming to you with hat in hand, you need to consider that saints learn from mistakes as sinners, and take each case on an individual basis. Establishing discipline does not necessarily require the command-and-control model used in the military. Training is a method of instilling discipline. The desire is to change the behavior of the person so that it matches the values of the organization.

---

[122] Ibid.

Captain D. Michael Abrashoff was the commanding officer of the USS *Benfold*, a modern destroyer in the US Navy fleet. He wrote an article, "Retention Through Redemption,"[123] about how he used the leadership concepts we have been discussing to turn around the crew of the *Benfold* and make it the highest-producing, most sought-after assignment in the Navy. When he took over the ship, the crew actually cheered and celebrated the previous commander's departure, so Captain Abrashoff really had his hands full.

Captain Abrashoff involved the crew in problem solving, accepted their input, implemented their ideas, and gained the support of the entire crew. He made it clear that they were all in it together. He listened to the crew and trusted them. He did all the things that Admiral Rogge did to show the crew he cared. He established discipline through trust and shared vision. He did maintain order and used punishment in moderation. Offenses were punished as necessary, but he continued to show the crew he cared by such actions as sitting down to play cards with two sailors he had restricted to the ship after a fight.

I had some officers who violated a pursuit policy in a way that put them in danger. I wanted them to understand how important discipline was in maintaining a safe environment during a pursuit. I gave them articles on discipline to read and asked them to report back to me with their thoughts. I completed the necessary employee discipline reports but also spent time with them discussing why this was important for them to understand. Both officers are supervisors now. I always sat down with the offending parties and explained what actions I was taking and why. It was not about punishment; these were opportunities to develop them and demonstrate care.

These are supposed to be learning events, but the choice of what to do afterward lies with the recipient of the action, whether the recipient is you or someone else. People must know there is forgiveness from you

---

123 Commander Abrashoff, D. Michael, "Redemption Through Retention," *Harvard Business Review*, February 2001.

and the organization. How employees accept disciplinary action is a direct indication of your power and ability to lead.

Imagine that you have a choice between two people; the first has a perfect record, and the second has made some mistakes but has excelled to overcome the errors. Who would you choose? If the person who fixes himself never gets a break, how long can he stay motivated? If the person who never fails at anything gets passed over, how long can she stay motivated? Remember, whatever action you take, you are sending messages to everyone in the organization. Think about the values you are using in this selection process.

Sexual Static

In most of the movies and examples we have discussed, the leaders are always male. This is unfortunate, but these examples are only meant to look at the leadership qualities, not the gender of the leader. In today's world, General Savage could be a female; Amazing Grace could be a woman basketball star, and Serpico, a female chief of police; Jaime Escalante is probably a female principal or college president, and the male CEOs are giving way to the Meg Whitmans. Women are leaders everywhere, in all professions.

The Sea Wolf is a very manly book of rough seamen and treacherous captains until they pick up Maude from a lifeboat in the open ocean. Things suddenly change aboard the *Ghost*, just as things change in the business world when women are present. It is not the women that change; it is the behavior of the men.

Judy Rosener said this best, "Both men and women experience sexual static. It causes frustration for women and discomfort for men. Women are frustrated because they feel the static could be minimized if men understood gender differences. Men just want the static to go away. They feel working with women means walking on eggshells and although they are not sure what causes the static, they know it is associated with the presence of women."[124]

---

[124] Rosener, Judy B., *America's Competitive Secrets* (New York: Oxford Press, 1995).

Many women are better at leadership than men. Women naturally tend to gravitate toward shared decision making, use of personal power, sharing power, choosing rather than deciding, organizational goals, and shared success. We have been discussing all of these as valued concepts in leadership.

There is good material out there for leaders of both sexes to read to help understand the issues that surface when women and men work together. Understanding the differences between men and women is important to being an effective leader. Rather than try to cover the topic here, I am going to recommend that you read some other material specifically directed to it.

In the leadership program, we used some excerpts from Judy Rosener's book, *America's Competitive Secrets*, but there is much more available, such as Deborah Tannen's *You Just Don't Understand,* John Gray's *Men Are from Mars, Women Are from Venus,* and so on. I feel it is important to discuss the issues and differences in the workplace. If we get these issues out in the open, then men and women will better understand the things that create sexual static. They will be more comfortable with each other and more productive.

That is not the way things happened on the *Ghost,* though. Maude is the catalyst for some serious changes involving Hump and Wolf—but you will have to read the book to understand all that!

Courage and Responsibility

As a final exercise in the course, we have the class members select a pair of concepts and prepare a presentation. There are many choices, as by then, we have discussed a lot of leadership concepts that fit into other concepts. The purpose is to show that the concepts are not separable and are tied together so that any one relates to all the others in some capacity. It is designed to show that the leader needs to have the whole picture in his or her head at all times.

To see what we have learned, let me ask you to review just a few of these basic concepts. Think about how they relate to each other and to leadership. If you can see the relationships, you may have learned more than you think.

- Communication and adult learning
- Confidence and a commitment to excellence
- Vision and empowerment
- Respect and power
- Developer mind-set and paradigms
- Perspectives and humility
- Professionalism and tenacity
- Discipline and loyalty
- Values and integrity
- Flexibility and focus
- Management skills and Theory Y
- Support and risk
- Courage and responsibility

I always wondered why, in *The Sea Wolf,* Wolf Larson allowed Humphrey Van Weyden to live and share the comforts he (Wolf) had. Many times Wolf and Hump had dinner conversations that were very intellectual, debating philosophy and the meaning of life. Wolf would dominate with his "only the fit deserve to survive" philosophy. It seemed like a game of cat and mouse, but I don't think Wolf was really looking to defeat and consume Hump; it was more like he was hoping that Hump could change, defeat, or consume him.

Wolf was self-taught. Everything he knew came from his reading and life experiences. I wonder, though, *had he really learned?* I believe Wolf was attempting to learn and either validate or challenge his paradigm in his talks with Hump. For experiential learning to occur, we need to be challenged and engaged in a process of discovery to find that aha moment. Wolf could not do that until Hump came on board; however, even with Hump to challenge him, he refused to allow himself to learn (think back to our learning discussions in chapter 1). It was very obvious that Hump was playing with fire each time he challenged and engaged Wolf. In the end, it was Wolf who was inadvertently developing courage and values in Hump that eventually enabled him to escape.

There are always temptations to take the easy way out of situations. On board the *Ghost*, life was tough and troubled. Several of the crew, such as Johnson and Leach, wanted to kill Wolf for being the beast he was. They made attempts but were always unsuccessful, as most of the crew was just too scared of Wolf to join in the attacks. I always read this passage from *The Sea Wolf* to the class on the last day. Wolf and Hump are having one of their discussions. This is Wolf talking to Hump:

> Of the two of us, you and I, who is the greater coward, he asked seriously. If the situation is unpleasing, you compromise with your conscience when you make yourself a party to it. If you were really great, really true to yourself, you would join forces with Leach and Johnson. But you are afraid, you are afraid. You want to live. The life that is in you cries out that it must live, no matter what the cost, so you live ignominiously, untrue to the best you dream of, sinning against your whole pitiful little code, and if there were a hell, heading your soul straight for it. Bah, I play the braver part. I do not sin, for I am true to the promptings of the life that is in me. I am sincere with my soul at least, and that is what you are not.[125]

Hump said that there was a sting in Wolf's words, as he felt the truth of the notion that failing to uphold one's convictions and values was cowardice. We do that everyday in picking our battles or just ignoring difficult situations in hopes they will work themselves out. Many times things do work out, but the concept-pairing presentation that was most impressive to me considered a time it did not. Situations like this occur in police work all the time, but they also occur in different ways in all forms of business, politics, government, and family,

I worked with an officer many years ago, when I started police work. He was a really outstanding person, who taught me a lot on many occasions when we were new officers working together. Later, after I had moved to another department and lost touch with him, we ended up together again, this time with him as a sergeant and a student in my class. When

---

125 London, *The Sea Wolf*, 123.

it came time for the concept pairings, he chose to present on courage and responsibility. He had to prepare a ten-minute presentation of how those concepts related to each other and to leadership. Of the many presentations that I experienced, this presentation impacted me the most, and I shared it with many a class at the end.

He had been the supervisor/sergeant of the narcotics unit in his department. He had a young officer working for him in narcotics who was an excellent, productive officer. This officer had one last case to work on before he was to transfer out of the unit to another assignment. This officer was also the sergeant's close friend—so close that the sergeant had been the best man at this officer's wedding.

The sergeant began his presentation by giving us all that background, and as he continued, we all came to realize we knew of the incident. The officer had arranged to make an undercover buy of drugs from a dealer in another county. The sergeant told us how there were warning signs that this deal was not going to go smoothly. The sergeant said he received calls and warnings from other supervisors and officers, begging him to stop the deal from going through. He discussed it with the officer, but the officer was also begging him, as his close friend, to let him finish this one last deal. The officer was sure he could make it work. The sergeant reluctantly agreed, fearing he might damage their friendship if he did what he thought he should do and put a stop to the transaction.

On the day of the deal, everyone was in place, and warning signs abounded, but the sergeant allowed the officer to continue. When the officer went in to make the deal, he was shot and killed in a rip-off by the dealer. All hell broke loose in the moments that followed as the other officers attempted to contain the situation and arrest the killers.

In his presentation the sergeant said, "This is how courage and responsibility relate to leadership: I did not have the courage to carry out my responsibility as the leader, and my best friend died as the result." He asked us if we could help him deal with that. His "ten-minute" presentation lasted over an hour, with all of us sobbing along with him. It was a *significant emotional event* that tattooed courage and responsibility forever in the hearts and minds of everyone present.

As leaders, there are many times when we see things but choose not to deal with the issues. I told you how compassionate Cunningham was toward me when I displayed my turmoil over having to actually be a supervisor and a leader, as that seemed to take the fun out of the job. But this is the job of the leader: to love your people, yet try not to allow them to hurt themselves, while developing them to excel beyond any limitations.

What Now?

I mentioned that I show *Mr. Holland's Opus* as the last movie in the leadership program. My reason is that Mr. Holland never starts out to be or ever considers himself to be a leader. He is just a guy who wants to write music, and then life happens to him.

Like all of us, he stumbles through life trying to raise a family and make a living, not really noticing the impact he has on others. He is a high school music teacher, at first by necessity, and then he learns how to teach. He begins to see that sharing his knowledge and caring about the kids works to make his own life happy. He forgets himself and dedicates his life to creating a work or a deed beyond himself, as Dr. Frankl explained in his book.

In doing so, Mr. Holland leaves a lifelong impact on the souls he has taught. At the end of the movie they all return to repay him that debt. If you don't cry when you watch this, you are much tougher than I. I believe it is one of the greatest leadership movies ever made. This fictional story of leadership is one that is repeated by caring, loving leaders every day: leaders who are developing people to excel beyond their limitations, teaching people to learn and think through music like Mr. Holland, through math like Jaime Escalante, or through any number of other mediums. They teach values in amazing ways without really trying.

Captain Joseph Charles (Charlie) Plumb was a fighter pilot who flew missions over North Vietnam during the Vietnam conflict. He was shot down in

1967 and held captive for the next six years as a POW. Captain Plumb wrote a book, *I'm No Hero* (though in reality he is), and does motivational speaking in many arenas. I learned about him from a student who showed me an article called "Lumps, Parachutes and Perspectives" by Special Agent Edward F. Sulzbach of the FBI Academy in Quantico, Virginia. This article related the parachute-packing story that Captain Plumb recounts in many of his speaking engagements (which I recommend you attend if you get an opportunity).

Since then, I have been to Captain Plumb's presentations, shown his videos for training, read his book, and had an opportunity to meet this true American hero. Captain Plumb has many stories about his life, but the best known is probably his parachute-packing story.

Captain Plumb was having dinner in a restaurant after being repatriated to the United States, following his six years as a POW in North Vietnam. A gentleman came over to him, pointed at him, and said, "You're Plumb." Captain Plumb asked him how he knew him. The man said, "I packed your parachute." Plumb asked him if he remembered all the chutes he packed, and the gentleman said, "Nope, just the ones that get used. I guess it worked!" Plumb said that he really shook the man's hand and sincerely thanked him.

Plumb said that he had thought about this man many times during his years of captivity, how he might have passed him often on board the aircraft carrier and never noticed him at all. And as Plumb was floating down from the sky into North Vietnam, he had realized just how important this man's work really had been, and how very thankful he was that the man had taken his job seriously.

Plumb said that he realized just how important his other parachutes were, like his mental parachute, spiritual parachute, and emotional parachute, all packed by his parents, coaches, ministers, naval academy instructors, teachers, and friends. All of these people had a role in preparing him for the six years of his life that he spent in captivity. They had a role in preparing him mentally, emotionally, physically, and spiritually to endure captivity and torture that most of us could never even imagine. But Plumb made it, along with many others who are pretty healthy and sane; they've done even better than some others who did not endure capture.

So back to the question: What now? Whose parachutes are you packing, and who is packing yours? You are a leader, you are visible, and you influence the values of everyone you come into contact with. Are you doing the best you can to prepare them, showing them you care, and helping them to excel? Are you still trying to learn? Are you arguing for your weaknesses? Have you done away with limitations? Do you realize all knowledge is incomplete?

Can you learn to be a better leader?

Afterword

In every decent work of leadership, the emphasis is on working on yourself while learning to lead others. Dr. Covey's seventh habit is to *"sharpen the saw."* It is a continual process. That is why books like *Zen and the Art of Motorcycle Maintenance, Jonathan Livingston Seagull, Man's Search for Meaning, Courageous Follower, The 7 Habits of Highly Effective People, Managing for Excellence, Leaders,* and *The Sea Wolf* provide such great insights that allow you to think about yourself. Lieutenant Cunningham always wanted this information shared with everyone. His goal (and mine) has always been to help create a better world and a hunger for more knowledge. At the end of the book I have listed recommended reading, much of which was used in the leadership course, so you can take advantage of these resources.

As you read through this book, I hope you saw how valuable it would be to read the suggested material and watch the movies in addition to reading this book. I am trying to point out bits and pieces of that additional material to maximize your potential learning. I believe you will see things in those books I never dreamed of, and those will be issues that also impact your life and learning.

Each class had a total of twenty-nine minds with between five hundred and eight hundred years of combined experience, knowledge, ideas, and learning to share with each other. When you add the years of additional knowledge contained in the books, movies, articles, and so on, you come out with an astronomical amount of information to draw upon. It will probably take you several hours to read this book, and if you add in the supplemental reading, you may end up with fifty or sixty hours of reading time. The time spent in class was 192 hours plus evening sessions and outside work, discussion time, and so on. Three hundred hours would not be an unreasonable estimate of the total time spent looking at thousands of years of knowledge on leadership.

The class time was spent in discussion and dialogue, exploration of concepts, exercises, presentations, and just the sheer joy of learning. Class time was fun; some classes had yellow (BS) penalty flags that were thrown by students. One class had a toy bus they would roll out when someone was "thrown under the bus"; other classes had other props. There were class activities such as barbecues and volleyball games to aid in team building and break up the barrage of information. Many students would tell me that they spent so much time thinking in class that their brains hurt and they were exhausted by the end of each session. Students said they drove home after three days without turning on the radio, because their brains were full of thoughts, and everything was still rattling around, making too much noise for them to entertain anything else.

I no longer teach in the leadership program. Most of the original instructors/facilitators have retired, and the program has been updated and changed to the point that most of this material is no longer used. I can tell you that the program was always highly effective.

Many executive officers would come to us at graduation and tell us they had seen dramatic changes in the people at work over the past few months. Many spouses would come to us in tears at graduation and say that they did not know what we had done to their loved ones over the past eight months, but that they had changed, and they were grateful for whatever it was we had done. But the students made the changes, not us. We just provided the opportunity; they controlled how they motivated themselves.

Almost every graduation was an emotional event. The classes tended to bond very tightly over the eight months, and those bonds lasted many years. People who had been through the course spoke to each other in a new language that was shared through the leadership program and aided in networking. Graduates terrorized other more traditional management training programs because they would tend to challenge the old methods of teaching and management.

The last session was presented entirely by the students, with projects and required final essays that covered an assortment of learning goals. We wanted to know how the learning goals impacted them. We wanted to know if the course had been successful and what they would change.

In one final paper, a student wrote that on the first day of class a sergeant was there who was overconfident and a know-it-all, who always had the "correct" opinion. As the sessions went on, that person was not as loud, was not there as often, and discovered he was wrong a lot. By the end of the course this sergeant was not present; he had ceased to exist, and a new person had shown up to take his place. Of course, he was talking about himself and how he made life-changing choices through the class. Often I was tired of butting heads with very stubborn people, but this was the kind of impact that inspired me to continue presenting in this course for many years and to write this book.

Sometimes I got calls from students a year after the class to tell me they finally understood something and to thank me. I ran into one guy a few years after he completed the program. He thanked me for helping him to understand that his whole life was a lie. He said that he had divorced his wife, dumped his girlfriend, and changed jobs. I was petrified. I quickly said that this had not been my intent. He just smiled, happily shaking my hand, and told me not to worry. It wasn't anything I did; it was something he finally was able to understand from all the events that had happened during class. He was a happy and changed person.

This book, like that course and anything else, is only what you make of it. Anytime you choose to go back and start reading the suggested books or just reread this one, you will be engaged in your own search to learn leadership; all of that is good. However, if you were to look me up and ask me to give a one-day seminar, the answer would be an unequivocal no; that would be a waste of your time and mine. To make changes in your life or in others, you need time to digest and understand, so you must commit to the long term.

Captain Dave Smith, from the Torrance Police Department in California, was my partner in instructing one class. In the last hour of the first session, we asked the group members for comments on the session. One student said that he was concerned that the heavy reading and class discussion time would be a waste of his time, and he wanted to know how we would compensate him for that since he was only here to get his ticket punched for promotion. I was about to stand up and address him when Dave pushed me down and began responding.

Dave explained that we put a lot of time into preparing for each session. We spent a lot of time reading book reviews, and the assortment of work they did. We devoted many hours to research, trying to improve our knowledge and the course itself. Dave explained to him that there are no shortcuts to take. Either he could make the commitment to the process, or leave right then and make room for others that wanted to learn. Our time was just as valuable as his.

Another student was annoyed that some concepts were discussed at length in the lobby/bar after class one night and wanted to know what was said. The class told her she should have been there, if she really wanted to be involved. She said it did not matter; her people did what she told them to because she was the boss and that she did not really care about them anyway.

My point in sharing this is to illustrate that not everyone is going to be a success story. Not everyone is going to be loved by his or her subordinates or managers. Not everyone is going to be a good leader. Some people are simply never going to be leaders because they choose not to be. The upside is that this leaves an opportunity to fill that gap. I had a mentor tell me to always take all the stuff no one wants, because soon you will have everything—and at some point they will want some back.

The end of this book is not the end, but the beginning of an opportunity to continue to learn and explore more areas of leadership. A frequent comment I got from past students was that this was a great course in leadership, but it was all "pie in the sky" concepts that would never work in the "real world." That sounds very cynical and weak to me. If you argue it won't work and you refuse to have the courage to try, you will be right. After the loss of a high school basketball game, Charlie Plumb told his coach that thought he was a loser. His coach replied, "If you think you are a loser, then you are." It is another lesson in the Pygmalion Effect, the self-fulfilling prophecy, dooming yourself to failure.

Other students said they were amazed at the results they got by following the concepts and making the necessary changes in their own lives. While we covered a lot of things, there is so much more to explore. Get into all the training and education that you can. Take chances and push past the limits that you have placed on yourself.

Fly, Jonathan, fly.

Recommended Supplemental Materials

Books

1. Charles J. Sykes, *A Nation of Victims*: *The Decay of the American Character*
2. Charlie Plumb, *I'm No Hero*
3. Dave Carey, *The Ways We Choose: Lessons from a POW's Experience*
4. David L. Bradford and Allan R. Cohen, *Managing for Excellence: The Guide to Developing High Performance in Contemporary Organizations*
5. Elaine Brown, *A Taste of Power: A Black Woman's Story*
6. Hugh Pearson, *The Shadow of the Panther: Huey Newton and the Price of Black Power in America*
7. Ira Chaleff, *The Courageous Follower*
8. Jack London, *The Sea Wolf*
9. James A. Michener, *Kent State: What Happened and Why*
10. James M. Jenks and John M. Kelly, *Don't Do, Delegate*
11. Jay Mathews, *Escalante: The Best Teacher in America*
12. Joshua Halberstam, *Everyday Ethics: Inspired Solutions to Real-Life Dilemmas*
13. Judy B. Rosener, *America's Competitive Secrets*
14. Malcolm Gladwell, *Blink: The Power of Thinking Without Thinking*
15. Neil Postman and Charles Weingartner, *Teaching as a Subversive Activity*
16. Niccolo Machiavelli, *The Prince*
17. Peter Drucker, *The Age of Discontinuity*

18. Peter Drucker, *The Practice of Management*
19. Peter M. Senge, *The Fifth Discipline: The Art and Practice of the Learning Organization*
20. Richard Bach, *Jonathan Livingston Seagull*
21. Robert M. Pirsig, *Zen and the Art of Motorcycle Maintenance: An Inquiry into Values*
22. Spencer Johnson, MD, *Who Moved My Cheese?*
23. Stephen Covey, *The 7 Habits of Highly Effective People*
24. Viktor E. Frankl, *Man's Search for Meaning: An Introduction into Logo Therapy*
25. W. Timothy Gallwey, *The Inner Game of Tennis*
26. Warren Bennis and Burt Nanus, *Leaders: The Strategies for Taking Charge*

Publications

1. Bernhard Rogge, Vice Admiral, Federal German Navy (retired), *Leadership Aboard the Raider Atlantis*, from *Proceedings*, copyright 1963 by US Naval Institute
2. CSM John M. Stevens, "Combat Ready," *Armor*, January–February 1984
3. CSM John M. Stevens, "First Impressions," *Armor*, November–December 1983
4. D. Michael Abrashoff, "Redemption Through Retention," *Harvard Business Review*, February 2001
5. Dan Carlson, "Hey, Who's Responsible for this Mess?," Fall 1994 The Washington Post Writers Group, The Ethics Roll Call
6. David A. Kolb, Adult Learning Theory
7. Debra Meyerson, *Tempered Radicals: How People Use Difference to Inspire Change at Work,* Cantola Productions, 2001
8. Karlene H. Roberts, Naval Institute Proceedings, in press, "Bishop Rock Dead Ahead, The Grounding of the *USS Enterprise*," University of California, Berkeley
9. Kenneth R. Andrews, "Ethics in Practice," *Harvard Business Review*, September–October 1989
10. Kermit Vandivier, "The Case of the Corporate Coward: The Great Aircraft Brake Scandal," *Harper's*, April 1972

11. Lt. Col. Zeb B. Bradford Jr., "Duty, Honor and Country vs. Moral Conviction," *Army Magazine*, September 1968
12. Luther Gulick, "Notes on the Theory of Organization," in *Papers on the Science of Administration*, ed. Luther Gulick and L. Urwick (New York: Institute of Public Administration, 1937)
13. Marshall Sashkin, PhD, Managerial Values Profile (MVP)
14. Michael Hyams, "Communicating the Ethical Standard," *Journal of California Law Enforcement*, 1991
15. Monika Byrd, Phi Theta Kappa, http://www.ptk.org/leaddev/news/item116.htm, March 2005
16. Richard Tanner Pascale, "Zen and the Art of Management," *Harvard Business Review*, March–April 1978
17. Robert Manning, "The World of Epictetus, Reflections on Survival and Leadership," *Atlantic Monthly*, 1978
18. Sam Crowell, "A New Way of Thinking: The Challenge for the Future," *Educational Leadership*, September 1989

Videos

1. *60 Minutes*, "A Matter of Honor," CBS
2. *The Abilene Paradox*, CRM
3. *The Constitution, That Delicate Balance*, "Criminal Justice and a Defendant's Right to a Fair Trial" (Episode 4), PBS
4. *What You Are Is Where You Were When*, Morris Massey, 1976

Movies

1. *Amazing Grace and Chuck*, Tri-Star Pictures, 1987
2. *Billy Budd*, Allied Artists, 1962
3. *The Caine Mutiny*, Columbia Pictures, 1954
4. *The Court-Martial of Billy Mitchell*, United States Pictures, 1955
5. *Mr. Holland's Opus*, Hollywood Pictures, 1995
6. *Patton*, Twentieth Century Fox, 1970
7. *Serpico*, Paramount Pictures, 1973
8. *Stand and Deliver*, Warner Bros Pictures, 1988
9. *Tunes of Glory*, United Artists, 1969
10. *Twelve O'Clock High*, Twentieth Century Fox Pictures, 1949

Open Book Editions
A Berrett-Koehler Partner

Open Book Editions is a joint venture between Berrett-Koehler Publishers and Author Solutions, the market leader in self-publishing. There are many more aspiring authors who share Berrett-Koehler's mission than we can sustainably publish. To serve these authors, Open Book Editions offers a comprehensive self-publishing opportunity.

A Shared Mission

Open Book Editions welcomes authors who share the Berrett-Koehler mission—Creating a World That Works for All. We believe that to truly create a better world, action is needed at all levels—individual, organizational, and societal. At the individual level, our publications help people align their lives with their values and with their aspirations for a better world. At the organizational level, we promote progressive leadership and management practices, socially responsible approaches to business, and humane and effective organizations. At the societal level, we publish content that advances social and economic justice, shared prosperity, sustainability, and new solutions to national and global issues.

Open Book Editions represents a new way to further the BK mission and expand our community. We look forward to helping more authors challenge conventional thinking, introduce new ideas, and foster positive change.

For more information, see the Open Book Editions website: http://www.iuniverse.com/Packages/OpenBookEditions.aspx

Join the BK Community! See exclusive author videos, join discussion groups, find out about upcoming events, read author blogs, and much more! http://bkcommunity.com/